Crossing Continents

Crossing Continents

*European Explorers and
India's Mysteries*

Amit Agarwal

ISBN: 978-93-6547-820-4

First published in India 2024
This edition published 2024

BluOne Ink Pvt. Ltd
A-76, 2nd Floor, Sector 136, Noida
Uttar Pradesh 201301
www.bluone.ink
publisher@bluone.ink

Kali, Occam and BluPrint are all trademarks of BluOne Ink Pvt. Ltd.

'This is indeed India ... the country of hundred nations and a hundred tongues, of a thousand religions and two million gods, cradle of the human race, birthplace of human speech, mother of history, grandmother of legend, great-grandmother of traditions, whose yesterday's bear date with the mouldering antiquities for the rest of nations – the one sole country under the sun that is endowed with an imperishable interest for alien prince and alien peasant, for lettered and ignorant, wise and fool, rich and poor, bond and free, the one land that all men desire to see, and having seen once, by even a glimpse, would not give that glimpse for the shows of all the rest of the world combined.'

—Mark Twain, *Following the Equator* (1897)

Contents

Acknowledgments

I wish to extend my sincere gratitude to everyone who supported and guided me in creating this book on European travellers to India. Crafting this book has been an enlightening journey of discovery and learning. This marks my fourth book, and through it, I can affirm that history showcases both the noblest and darkest aspects of human nature.

Foremost, I am deeply thankful to the travellers whose invaluable contributions formed the bedrock of this book. Your dedication to preserving and illuminating the history of European travel to India has served as an endless source of inspiration. I am indebted to the online libraries, archives and museums that grant access to rare manuscripts, documents and artefacts.

I express my sincere appreciation to my family and friends for their unwavering support and understanding during the extensive hours of research and writing. Your encouragement kept me motivated throughout this endeavour. As always, this book is dedicated to my parents, Ramesh and Sushil, who provided me with ample resources and freedom during my formative years, enabling me to think differently. My wife, Swati, encouraged me to embark on the journey of writing my first book, though she now graciously accepts that the majority of my time is dedicated to reading and writing. Similar to my previous works, my daughter, Eti, undertook the task of proofreading and creating numerous illustrations. Her keen eye for detail and commitment to excellence significantly enhanced the quality of this work.

I also express my gratitude to my boss Anurag Swarup, who motivated me throughout this journey. Credit is also due to my assistant, Ritu Verma, who diligently handled a significant portion of the office tasks, alleviating much of the workload from my shoulders.

I extend special thanks to my editor and the publishing team of BluOne Ink led by Praveen Tiwari for their expertise, guidance and dedication to bringing this book to publication. Your insightful contributions and unwavering commitment to the project were truly invaluable.

I extend my gratitude to Rajni Saini, a proficient dentist in London, who dedicated numerous hours to meticulously proofread every page, ensuring flawless grammar, spelling and the smooth flow of the story.

Lastly, I am profoundly grateful to the readers who share a passion for history and the tales of those fearless European travellers. Your interest in this book gives it purpose and relevance. This work stands as a testament to the collaborative effort of many, and I am humbled by the collective contributions that have shaped its pages.

Thank you all for being a part of this endeavour to illuminate the journeys, adventures and discoveries of European travellers to India.

Author's Note

Herodotus, a Greek historian in 450 BCE, often referred to as the 'Father of History', stated that India was the wealthiest and most populous country on earth. The Europeans' fascination with the land beyond the Indus River indeed has deep historical roots. The land, known variably as Bharat, Aryavart, Jambudweep, India, boasts a rich history and serves as a melting pot of diverse cultures, traditions and religions. The allure of India in European minds traces back to ancient times, from the trading hubs of the Harappan civilization to events like Greek invasions and extensive trade connections with Rome.

With India teeming with wealth and boasting open borders, individuals of all kinds – be they pure travellers, deeply religious maulvis, missionaries, traders or invaders – sought to bask in its glory and claim their share of the riches. The Silk Route, for instance, attracted numerous travellers to the vicinity of 'India', while Chinese explorers were drawn by the mystical allure of the land. Whereas, during the medieval era, invaders such as Qasim, Ghazni and Ghori embarked on perilous expeditions to plunder India's wealth and strip the country to the bone. During the zenith of Muslim rule in India, travellers from distant lands like Morocco arrived to observe. Many of them were displeased with the syncretic version of Islam and openly urged the sultans to enforce a stricter interpretation of the faith.

For the first time, Europe gained tangible information about India when Alexander attacked India in 326 BCE. Prior to that, India was more of a subject in Greek ballads than in historical or geographical texts. India was perceived as a land of abundance, a fact that attracted Europeans of all backgrounds. Unlike Arabs and Turks, Europeans were somewhat more sophisticated and initially persuaded trade and travel to gain insights into India.

Upon realizing that even during the Mughal rule, India remained an open *khazana*, they began spreading their wings, first by stationing small battalions of armed forces in their trading posts, and then gradually acquiring territory, inch by inch, foot by foot. India retained its status as the wealthiest country until 1700 CE, long after the British arrived. Subsequently, it was they who looted an estimated $45 trillion from India within just two centuries, leaving it impoverished. European dominion over India was established on the groundwork laid by these traders and travellers, whom we are about to discuss.

During the medieval era, European travellers undertook remarkable journeys to India, providing authentic chronicles of Indian history. These courageous explorers, motivated by a thirst for knowledge, trade opportunities or simply wanderlust, departed from their homelands, often without parental consent, to venture into the rich, exotic and mysterious land of India. These travellers confronted perilous journeys fraught with challenges, including marauding gangs, harsh climates, unfamiliar diseases, treacherous terrains and cultural disparities. Nonetheless, their eagerness to explore India's distant and exotic landscapes propelled them onward.

Cosmas Indicopleustes (literal translation, 'Cosmas who sailed to India'), hailing from Egypt, Africa, was the first Christian explorer to reach India in the 540s CE. Marco Polo, an Italian explorer who arrived in India in the late 13th century, stands as one of the earliest and most renowned medieval European travellers to India. His travelogue, *The Travels of Marco Polo*, offered invaluable insights into India's vibrant culture, diverse geography, complex political system and extensive trade networks to Europeans. Polo was captivated by the opulence of Indian cities such as Calicut and Cambay and detailed the thriving spice trade that attracted Europeans to the East. He played a pivotal role in igniting Europe's fascination with this distant realm during the medieval era. Similarly, in the early 15th century, Venetian merchant Niccolò de' Conti embarked on a journey to India. His accounts contributed to European understanding of India's diverse cultures, customs and wealth.

These early medieval European visitors to India laid the groundwork for subsequent European exploration and the establishment of trade routes connecting the East and the West. Their writings not only enriched European understanding of India but also sparked the imaginations of countless others, inspiring future generations of explorers, traders and adventurers to venture forth and contribute to the ever-expanding tapestry of global history.

In contrast, while Hindu merchants meticulously recorded their transactions, they did not document other aspects of life. One of the most prominent Indian texts, the *Arthashastra* of Kautilya, provides insights into politics, statecraft and economics, thereby shedding light on India's history. Additionally, the Puranas are increasingly considered as historical texts, offering valuable glimpses into India's past. However, apart from these limited accounts, Indians did not extensively document their history, which allowed others to shape historical narratives as they deemed fit.

Nearly all of our knowledge about India from the medieval era comes from foreign sources, including accounts by travellers like Polo, Manucci and Tavernier. Additionally, earlier figures such as Pliny (23–79 CE), an administrator for the Roman emperor Vespasian, wrote his pivotal book, *Naturalis Historia*, which contained valuable information about trade relations between India and the Roman Empire, with Pliny even accusing India of draining Rome's wealth during the first millennium. Before him, the Greek historian Megasthenes's work *Indica* provided insights into the Hindu way of life as well as the social, political and religious ecosystem of India. During the reign of Chandragupta II, the Chinese traveller Faxian documented India's religious landscape in his travelogue, *A Record of Buddhistic Kingdoms*, in the early 5th century. Another Chinese traveller, Hiuen Tsang (630–45 CE), elaborated on Indian society in his treatise *Si-Yu-Ki*.

This book endeavours to extract Indian history from the accounts of European travellers who visited India during the medieval period and wrote about their experiences, albeit through the lens of their biased Christian perspectives. Despite the multitude of travellers, only a select few have been chosen for inclusion, primarily due to space constraints within the book and partly because of their relative obscurity. These lesser-known travellers, not bound by the mandates of their rulers to report in a certain way, offer unique insights that merit exploration. It is imperative to recount their stories.

Stanley Lane-Poole, author of *Medieval India: Under Mohammedan Rule*, commented on the relevance of such travellers, stating, 'In such a cloud of witnesses of varied ranks, professions, and nationalities, truth, divested of insular or continental prejudice, may surely be found.' The wealth of information provided by their journals, letters and travels is indeed invaluable to the historian studying India.

After researching these travellers, certain common themes emerged in their writings. All of them were Christians and, hence, entirely comfortable with Muslims. However, they often faced pressure to convert to Islam during their time in India. The notable exception was the American traveller Mark Twain, who did not face such challenges as he visited during the peak of the British Empire. Furthermore, these travellers often expressed disapproval of the Hindu way of life, especially the worship of Hindu gods and the caste system, as well as practices such as nudity and sati. However, they also sympathized with the mistreatment of Hindus by Muslims. It is evident that these preferences and aversions persist to the present day.

Despite being ordinary individuals, all these travellers gained relatively easy access to Muslim rulers, primarily due to their 'Caucasian' appearance. Many of them were intrigued by the large number of women in Mughal harems. A few, such as William Hawkins and Manucci, even had privileged access, allowing them to witness firsthand the debauchery of the Muslim elite. Manucci and Tavernier also discussed the horrors and brutality of the Goa Inquisition unleashed by Portuguese Christians in which lakhs of Hindus were tortured to death over three centuries. These accounts would shock even the Turks.

Another common trait among these travellers was that they all recorded their observations in published books. A few, like Manucci and Tavernier, even adorned their work with beautiful illustrations depicting Indian life. These books provide comprehensive and rich accounts of their journeys in India and are regarded as seminal works in the genre of travel literature.

Despite not being professional authors or intellectuals, these travellers keenly observed their surroundings and felt compelled to share their experiences through writing. While their books often contained spelling and grammatical errors and were prone to repetitions, their content was compelling, interesting and truthful, leading many of them to become bestsellers.

Before criticizing their works for any dogmatism, it's essential to recognize the context of their religious upbringing, thought processes and writing styles. Their historical narratives should be studied while considering these factors, rather than imposing contemporary moral standards on the past.

In comparison, writings by Muslim travellers, with the exception of Al-Biruni, often appear one-dimensional, focussing heavily on praise for Islam, sultans, military prowess, wealth and harem life. Europeans' accounts, despite their biases and occasional bigotry, offer a fresher perspective. They provide sharper and more vivid depictions of India's reality.

A cotton plant as imagined by Sir John Mandeville.[1]

For instance, before the medieval era, India was perceived by Europeans as a wonderland of honey, milk and, of course, prized cotton. Nothing illustrates this better than *The Travels of Sir John Mandeville*, a fictitious account written between 1357 and 1371, purporting to describe a man's journey through Asia and India. One notable aspect of this work is Mandeville's portrayal of cotton plants, which he describes as resembling sheep sprouting from the ground and hanging low enough for grazing.. The popularity of the book can be gauged by the fact that it was translated into ten medieval European languages. Christopher Columbus even used it as a reference while planning his expedition to India. However, by the time William Hawkins embarked on his journey in the 1600s, India had already started to lose its aura of mystery.

The book, *Crossing Continents*, seeks to narrate the most noteworthy phases and extraordinary journeys in the lives of these travellers. It achieves this by weaving together their tales and insights, allowing readers to explore a bygone era. This book vividly portrays the cruel sultans, arrogant nobles, influential leaders, unscrupulous miners, superstitious diamond traders, zealous outlaws, dishonest political figures, common hapless citizens and captivating women, bringing them to life on the pages. Readers will feel as though they are witnessing history unfold before their eyes. The lifestyle of people, especially kings, wazirs and governors, is depicted as rich yet decadent. The book delves into the touching tales of travellers who often spent several years, and in some cases even decades, journeying across the 'mystical' cultural landscape of Europe, Asia, Africa and the adjacent seas and oceans, providing a comprehensive view of their experiences.

Additionally, the book also aims to retrace the paths taken by these travellers and their perceptive observations about a world that has faded over time. The objective is to provide the perspective of fortunate witnesses to India's historical and cultural richness while also shedding light on the challenges that afflicted the country, with the aim of offering valuable lessons. Amidst these pages, readers will also find glimpses of the everyday lives of ordinary people.

Bon Voyage!

1

The History of Travel Writing

Travel is fatal to prejudice, bigotry and narrow-mindedness.

The history of travel writing is indeed rich and diverse, spanning centuries and cultures. The tradition is ancient, with narratives such as Gilgamesh, an ancient Mesopotamian mythology dating back to the late 2nd millennium BCE, and Homer's *Odyssey*, an ancient Greek poem from the 7th century BCE, remaining significant to us even after thousands of years. These works tell the tale of the wanderer, positioned as an outsider who navigates existence without a clearly defined social role. The essence of travel writing lies in shedding preconceived notions and embracing the unknown. The more the traveller leaves behind the baggage of biases and assumptions, the more astute and insightful their observations become.

Travel writing embodies a distinctive form of historical documentation. Throughout history, humans have felt a compelling urge to travel, driven by various needs or simply by the innate curiosity inherent in all individuals. Travellers are unique individuals with diverse responses, motives, goals and enthusiasms. By their very nature, travellers are often free spirits, individuals who are motivated by a desire to explore the unknown rather than by ambitions of power or financial gain. They seek to understand what lies beyond the frontier, guided by a fascination for exploration and discovery.

India, much like history itself, harboured an entirely different notion about travel writing compared to the Western world. It wasn't shaped in the same mould as its Western counterpart. Instead, ancient Indian travel writing possessed a unique form, boasting a rich and diverse history, with notable contributions dating back to classical Sanskrit literature. While primarily focussed on statecraft and economics, the *Arthashastra* also contains chapters on governance and diplomacy, touching upon travel and interactions with foreign lands. Buddhist scriptures, particularly the Pali Canon, contain accounts of Buddha's journeys and those of his disciples. These writings meticulously detail the places visited during their quests to spread the teachings of Buddhism. The Sangam literature of ancient Tamil Nadu includes poems vividly depicting the experiences of seafaring traders, emphasizing maritime trade and cultural exchanges with distant lands. Legend has it that Adi Shankaracharya engaged in numerous philosophical debates with scholars from various schools of thought during his travels across India. These debates purportedly occurred in locations like Varanasi, Mahishmati (modern-day Maheshwar) and other towns, where he interacted with scholars representing diverse philosophical traditions. Multiple writings document these profound journeys.

Due to the inherent risks involved, there are no recorded accounts of women travellers. It wasn't until the late 18th century, with the emergence of modern means of communication, that women dared to venture into the vast and unknown regions of the world.

Throughout history, travel writing has fulfilled diverse purposes, including exploration, cultural exchange, education and entertainment. It persists in evolving, adapting to the changing ways in which people perceive and engage with the world.

2

Early European Knowledge of India

*'The Sanskrit language, whatever be its antiquity is of wonderful
structure, more perfect than the Greek, more copious than the Latin and
more exquisitely refined than either.'*

—William Jones

History indicates that for millennia, people worldwide have
used names derived from the Indus River, known as Sindhu
in Indian languages, to refer to the land now known as Bharat
or India. Examples include Hodu from the 'Book of Esther'
in the Bible, Indoi or Indou from ancient Rome, Hindustan from
the Persians, al-Hind or Indostan from the Arabs, Gyagar and
Phagyul from Tibet, and Tianzhú from China. Indians themselves
employed various names such as Aryavart, Jambudweep and
Bharat to denote their sacred lands.

In 2022, a 6-foot-tall Buddha statue, dating back to between
90 and 140 CE, was found at the ancient Roman port of Berenike
(now in Egypt) within the temple of Goddess Isis. This discovery
marks the first instance of a Buddha statue being found west of
Afghanistan. Inscriptions in Sanskrit dating to the reign of Roman
Emperor Philip the Arab (244–49 CE) and coins from the
Satavahana dynasty of the 2nd century CE were also discovered in

A Buddha statue found in Berenike, Egypt, dated 2nd century CE.[1]

the vicinity. These findings shed light on the extensive trade between India and Rome during ancient times.

In 440 BCE, Herodotus, a Greek historian and geographer, described India as the wealthiest and most populous country on earth. In his seminal work, *The Histories*, he enthused, 'Of all the inhabitants of Asia ... the Indians dwell nearest to the east and the rising of the Sun.... This is a great thing in India, that all are free, not a single Indian being a slave.'[2]

Following Alexander's conquest in 326 BCE, Greek historians like Megasthenes and Strabo provided detailed descriptions of Indian society, culture and geography. Megasthenes, who served as an ambassador to the court of Mauryan emperor Chandragupta Maurya, or, as some contemporary scholars suggest, to the court of Gupta emperor Chandragupta, extensively documented Indian politics, economy and social customs in his work *Indica*.

The Periplus of the Erythraean Sea, published in the mid-1st century CE, conveyed knowledge of the existence of the Guzerat and Malabar ports as well as of Masulipatam on the Coromandel coast and 'the Gangetic Mart' at the head of the 'great bay' of Bengal. It also referenced an explorer named Hippalus, who departed from the mouth of the Arabian Gulf and was propelled by the southwestern monsoon to Muziris (modern-day Mangalore), a port in Malabar.[3]

Pliny the Elder, a Roman author, naturalist and philosopher during the 1st century CE, wrote, 'In no year does India drain our empire of less than five hundred and fifty millions of sesterces, giving back her own wares in exchange, which are sold [among us] at fully one hundred times their prime cost.'[4] He expressed exasperation, noting that Roman women were particularly fond of Indian silk, gems, herbs, indigo and other exotic goods, lamenting, 'Why can't they be just happy with Roman wool?'[5]

In return, Indians primarily purchased items such as Roman wines, olive oil and similar commodities. At the height of this trade, approximately 120 Roman ships traversed between the Indian ports of Muziris and Bharuch and the Roman ports of Arsinoe, Berenice and Myos Hormos (now located in Egypt). India stands out as the sole recipient of thousands of ancient Roman coins, a distinction unmatched by any other country. Additionally, various Roman artefacts, including glassware, ceramics and bronze statuettes, have been unearthed from different parts of India. Notable among these discoveries is a miniature statue of Poseidon found in Kolhapur, Maharashtra.

At the opposite end of this exchange, Pompeii Lakshmi, an ivory statuette, was unearthed in the ruins of Pompeii, Italy, which was destroyed in the eruption of Mount Vesuvius in 79 CE. The statuette originated from the Gandhara region of India, dating back to the 1st century. It served as another perfect example of the interchange of ideas and culture between these two mighty civilizations.[6]

A valuable document known as the *Muziris Papyrus*, dating back to the 2nd century CE, was discovered, providing unparalleled insights into the ancient trade relationship between Roman Egypt and India. This document was a shipping contract crafted by a ship owner in Alexandria for a supplier in Kerala. It meticulously outlined the contents of the containers, insurance details and the legal contingencies in the event of a shipwreck.

One documented shipment from Muziris to Alexandria included approximately 790 pounds of textiles, 4,700 pounds of ivory and 700–1,700 pounds of nard, an aromatic balsam. This cargo was assessed at a total value of 131 talents, equivalent to the purchasing power of 2,400 acres of prime farmland in Egypt. Pliny's estimation becomes entirely plausible when one considers that a typical Roman cargo ship could accommodate approximately 150 such consignments.[7]

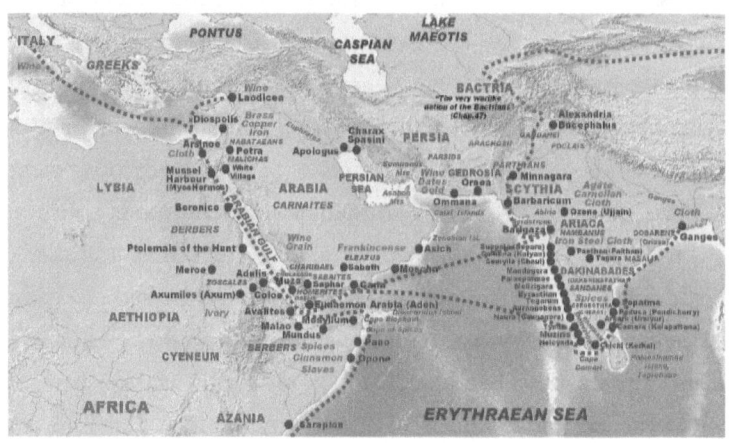

Indo-Roman trade route.[8]

Another contract documented in the *Muziris Papyrus* outlined a shipment weighing over 250 tonnes, comprising 167 elephant tusks, 80 boxes of spikenard and 140 tonnes of pepper. This cargo set sail on a Hermapollon boat destined for Alexandria. Departing from India, it made its way to the Myos Hormos port on the Red Sea. Upon reaching Myos Hormos, the cargo was unloaded and transported by camel through the Sahara to the Coptos port on the Nile. From there, it embarked on a ten-day journey downriver to Alexandria. This process of loading and unloading the ships, as well as the overland journey across the desert, required significant effort and resources, including a large number of camels and camel drivers, rendering it a challenging and costly operation. However, the value of the cargo, valued at approximately 6,911,852 drachmas (equivalent to 23–28 metric tonnes of silver), more than covered the transportation expenses.

The bustling ancient Sahara likely witnessed a multitude of desert caravans and river convoys laden with products if 120 vessels were unloading in Egypt each year. Berenike's substantial urban population, for its sustenance, necessitated at least 2,000 camel-loads of food per month. The 350-km desert route was made viable only through state subsidies for maintenance and infrastructure, which facilitated the transportation of covered Indian goods. In Alexandria (now in Egypt) and Rome, numerous corporate unions and guilds specialized in spices and aromatics. A typical pepper warehouse in Rome stored an estimated 9,000 tonnes of dry spices, safeguarded by military personnel.[9]

A gold coin of Claudius (50–51 CE) excavated in south India.[10]	A coin of Trajan, found together with coins of the Kushan ruler Kanishka, at the Ahin Posh Buddhist Monastery, Afghanistan.[11]

Ptolemy, the Greek geographer, provides extensive information on India in his work and demonstrates a profound understanding of its topography. Ptolemy's 'Tables' show that by 150 CE, traders were acquainted with the ports situated on both sides of the Bay of Bengal.[12]

Even following the decline of the Roman Empire after its conversion to Christianity, trade with India persisted, albeit to a much lesser extent. The final blow to this trade came when the Middle East fell under the Arab control, leading to the Arab domination of the distribution of goods from India to the Levant region (including present-day Jordan, Syria, Lebanon, etc.) of the Middle East. The imposition of heavy taxes resulted in goods becoming prohibitively expensive, diminishing their desirability in Europe.

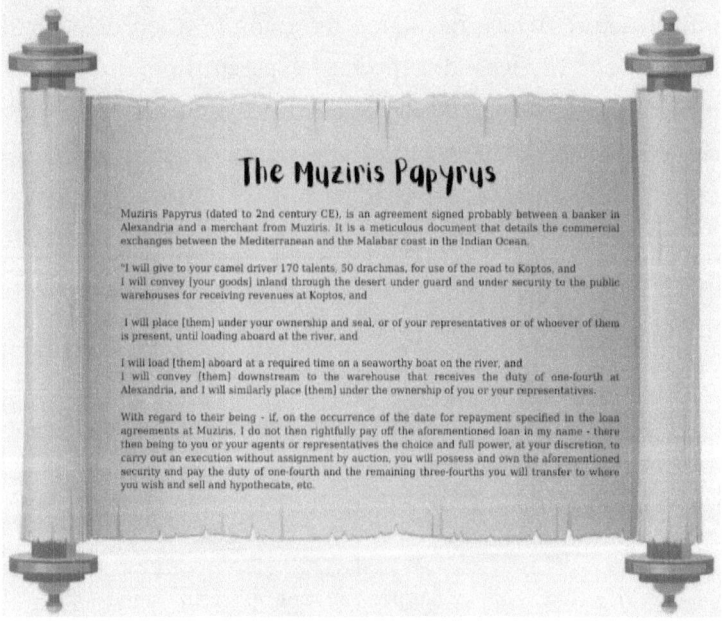

The Muziris Papyrus

Muziris Papyrus (dated to 2nd century CE), is an agreement signed probably between a banker in Alexandria and a merchant from Muziris. It is a meticulous document that details the commercial exchanges between the Mediterranean and the Malabar coast in the Indian Ocean.

"I will give to your camel driver 170 talents, 50 drachmas, for use of the road to Koptos, and I will convey [your goods] inland through the desert under guard and under security to the public warehouses for receiving revenues at Koptos, and

I will place [them] under your ownership and seal, or of your representatives or of whoever of them is present, until loading aboard at the river, and

I will load [them] aboard at a required time on a seaworthy boat on the river, and I will convey [them] downstream to the warehouse that receives the duty of one-fourth at Alexandria, and I will similarly place [them] under the ownership of you or your representatives.

With regard to their being – if, on the occurrence of the date for repayment specified in the loan agreements at Muziris, I do not then rightfully pay off the aforementioned loan in my name – there then being to you or your agents or representatives the choice and full power, at your discretion, to carry out an execution without assignment by auction, you will possess and own the aforementioned security and pay the duty of one-fourth and the remaining three-fourths you will transfer to where you wish and sell and hypothecate, etc.

Muziris Papyrus.[13]

However, Arab navies continued trading within Indian waters to such an extent that the fictionalized tales of 'Sindbad, the Sailor' were crafted, drawing inspiration from the experiences of Arab merchants in India.

Throughout the Middle Ages, European perceptions of India were largely shaped by the narratives of travellers and merchants like Marco Polo, who journeyed to India in the 13th century and documented its opulence and grandeur. However, it was the age of exploration during the 15th and 16th centuries that fostered a deeper understanding of India among Europeans.

Portuguese explorers like Vasco da Gama and Pedro Álvares Cabral were among the pioneers in establishing direct sea routes to India, thereby forging new pathways for trade and cultural exchange. Their expeditions also resulted in the establishment of Portuguese colonies in India, with Goa standing out as the most notable among them.

The Portuguese arrival in India was succeeded by other European powers, including the Dutch, French and British, who likewise established trading outposts and colonies in the region. Of these, the British East India Company (EIC) emerged as a dominant force, exerting substantial influence over large swathes of the subcontinent through its extensive trade networks and administrative authority.

Francois Bernier, a French physician who served in the durbar of Aurangzeb, believed that India represented the final destination for all the wealth in the world, even during the later years of the Mughal period. According to him, the gold and silver, having circulated through various regions across the globe, ultimately found their way to be absorbed in 'Hindostan'.[14] Bernier also mentioned the practice of burying gold and silver in the earth to safeguard it from falling into the hands of invaders. However, he observed that this act of putting precious metals out of circulation contributed to significant poverty within the country, despite India being abundant with wealth in the form of gold and silver.[15]

European fascination with India transcended mere trade and commerce; it encompassed a profound interest in the study of Indian languages, religions and philosophies. Scholars like William Jones made remarkable contributions to the study of Sanskrit and the translation of ancient Indian texts, thereby enriching European understanding of Indian culture and civilization.

Overall, early European knowledge of India was shaped by a complex interplay of trade, exploration and cultural exchange. These interactions laid the foundation for future relations between Europe and India, contributing to a deeper understanding and appreciation, while sometimes also leading to misinterpretations or even denigration of Indian society and culture in the Western world. The motives of religion, race and commerce often tainted the minds and works of European travellers, especially during the medieval era. Such biases sometimes clouded their observations of Indian society and culture.

3

Prominent Foreign Travellers to India

'India conquered and dominated China for 20 centuries without ever having to send a single soldier across its border.'
—Hu Shih, former Chinese ambassador to USA

Megasthenes (302–298 BCE)

- He was a Greek envoy and scholar.
- He was sent by Seleucus Nicator, a Greek general and successor of Alexander the Great, as an ambassador to the court of Chandragupta Maurya.
- His work *Indica* provided an account of India, although the original manuscript is lost. Fragments of his writings have survived through quotations by other authors.
- He wrote about serving in the durbar of Sandracottus. However, William Jones, an 18th-century scholar of ancient India, erroneously identified Sandracottus as Chandragupta Maurya of the 3rd century BCE, when he was actually referring to Chandragupta of the Gupta dynasty of the 4th century CE. Both Chandraguptas lived around seven centuries apart, and this misinterpretation distorted the chronology of Indian history.

- He meticulously documented India's significant rivers, including the Sindhu and Ganga, in his writings.
- Often hailed as the 'Father of Indian History', Megasthenes holds the distinction of being the first foreigner to write extensively about ancient India.

Deimachos (320–273 BCE)

- He was a Greek envoy who succeeded Megasthenes.
- He was sent by Antiochus I, the son of Seleucus Nicator, to Bindusara or Amitraghata, the successor of Chandragupta Maurya.
- He provided crucial insights into the society and politics of ancient India.
- Although Deimachos wrote extensively on India, his works have unfortunately been lost to history.

Ptolemy (90–168 CE)

- He was a citizen of Roman Egypt who wrote in Greek.
- His notable work, *The Geography of India*, offered a detailed portrayal of the geography of ancient India.
- According to Ptolemy, one of the most notable features of India is its shape, characterized by the acute angle formed by the peninsula's two coastlines merging to form a single coastline that stretches nearly from the mouth of the Indus to the mouth of the Ganges.

Faxian (405–11 CE)

- The Chinese traveller journeyed to India on foot during the reign of Chandragupta Vikramaditya.
- Faxian holds the distinction of being the first Buddhist pilgrim to visit India.

- He provided vital information about the Gupta dynasty as well as the social and economic landscape of India during his travels.
- Faxian is well-known for his pilgrimage to Lumbini, the birthplace of Buddha.
- His journey is chronicled in his travelogue titled *A Record of Buddhist Kingdoms*.

Xuanzang (630 CE)

- The Chinese traveller visited India and stayed here for fifteen years during the reign of Harsh Vardhan.
- Xuanzang extensively researched the caste structure prevalent during his time in India and documented his findings in the book *Si-Yu-Ki* (*The Records of the Western World*).
- Upon his return, Xuanzang brought back over six hundred Mahayana and Hinayana texts, along with seven Buddha statues and over a hundred Buddhist relics.

I-Tsing (671–95 CE)

- He was a Chinese traveller who journeyed to Nalanda in India to study Buddhism.
- Notably, he was the only Chinese traveller to reach India via the sea route, stopping at Srivijaya in Indonesia during his voyage.
- His prominent contributions include biographies of several famous monks.
- I-Tsing played a significant role in translating many Buddhist texts from Sanskrit and Pali into Chinese.

Al-Masudi (957 CE)

- He was an Arab traveller.
- He was referred to as the 'Herodotus of the Arabs'.

- In his book, *Muruj-ul-Zehab*, he gives an account of India, which also integrates scientific geography, social commentary and biographies within the framework of universal history.
- The book examines India's political, economic and religious histories.

Al-Biruni (1024–30 CE)

- He was a Persian scholar.
- He accompanied Mahmud of Ghazni to India.
- He is regarded as the first Muslim scholar to travel to India for study purposes.
- He authored the book *Tārīkh al-Hind* (*The History of India*).
- He is often hailed as the 'Father of Indology'.
- He meticulously explored the cultural, scientific and religious aspects of Hindu life, documenting the secular and academic dimensions of Hindu society.
- He studied religion within the context of a vibrant culture milieu.

Marco Polo (1292–94 CE)

- He was an Italian mercantile businessman and explorer.
- He visited south India during the reign of Madurai's Pandyan emperor, Madverman Kulshekhara (1272–1311), and Rudramma Devi of the Kakatiyas.
- His renowned work, *The Travels of Marco Polo*, provides a comprehensive overview of India's economic history.

Ibn Battuta (1333 to 1342 CE)

- He was a Moroccan traveller.
- He visited India during the reign of Muhammad bin Tughlaq.
- He was appointed as a judge by Tughlaq.

- His work, *The Travels*, provides insights into the much-maligned administrative reforms of Delhi Sultan Muhammad bin Tughlaq.
- His book *Rihla* served as a travelogue documenting his journeys.
- He holds the record for travelling more extensively than any other explorer in pre-modern history, covering approximately 117,000 km.

Shihabuddin al-Umari (1348 CE)

- He was an Arab from Damascus.
- In his book, *Masalik Albsar fi-mamalik Al-Amsar*, he offers a detailed description of India, including accounts from Odoric of Pordenone, a Franciscan friar and missionary explorer.
- He observed that during Alauddin Khilji's rule from 1296 to 1316, the sale of thousands of slaves occurred daily.

Nicolo Conti (1420–21 CE)

- He was a Venetian traveller.
- He arrived during the reign of Devraya I of the Sangam dynasty of the Vijayanagar Empire.
- He provided a graphic representation of Vijayanagar's capital.
- He also contributed to the creation of the Fra Mauro map in 1450, which hinted at the possibility of a sea route from Europe around Africa to India. The map mentions the travels of a 'Zoncho de India', likely a reference to a 'junk' (Chinese sailing ship) from India, which could indicate China or Southeast Asia, both considered part of Greater India at the time.

Abdur Razzaq (1443–44 CE)

- He was a Persian traveller and ambassador serving under Shahrukh of the Timurid dynasty.

- His travels coincided with the reign of Devraya II of the Vijayanagar Empire, during which he provided vivid descriptions of its enormous wealth and grandeur.
- While in India, he stayed at the palace of the Zamorin of Kozhikode in Calicut.
- His notable work, *Matla-us-Sadain wa Majma-ul-Bahrain*, offers detailed accounts of life and events during the reign of the Zamorin in Calicut as well as insights into the ancient city of Vijayanagar at Hampi.
- Abdur Razzaq also documented the maritime trade in the Indian Ocean during the 15th century.

Afanasy Nikitin (1470–74 CE)

- He was a Russian businessman, who travelled to south India.
- He provides accounts of the Bahmani kingdom during the reign of Muhammad III (1463–82).
- His narrative, *Journey beyond Three Seas*, was lost until rediscovered in the 18th century. It served as the inspiration for a Hindi movie, *Pardesi*, based on his travels.

Duarte Barbosa (1500 CE)

- He was a Portuguese traveller.
- He resided in India for sixteen years, with the majority of his time spent in Kerala under the Vijayanagar Empire.
- Barbosa extensively studied Malayalam and documented the caste culture and social life in the region.
- Afonso de Albuquerque, the viceroy of Portugal in Goa, employed Barbosa's linguistic skills as an interpreter in an unsuccessful attempt to convert the king of Kochi.
- He authored the *Book of Duarte Barbosa*.

Domingo Paes (1520–22 CE)

- He was a traveller from Portugal who visited the court of Krishnadeva Raya of the Tuluv dynasty in the Vijayanagar Empire.
- He documented advanced irrigation techniques employed by the kingdom, enabling the production of high crop yields at reasonable prices.
- Paes described the wealth of Hampi to the extent that diamonds were reportedly sold on the streets.

Fernao Nuniz (1535–37 CE)

- He was a Portuguese horse trader who, at one point, evaded the Inquisition and openly lived as a Jew in Constantinople, within the Ottoman Empire.
- He visited India during the reign of Achyutdeva Raya of the Tuluv dynasty in the Vijayanagar Empire.
- He wrote a comprehensive history of the empire, chronicling its origins and development from inception.

John Hughen Von Linschotten (1563 CE)

- He was probably the only traveller from the Netherlands during this time.
- Dubbed as the Dutch Marco Polo, he reached Goa in 1563.
- He offered significant insights into the social and economic landscape of south India, especially regarding the Vijayanagar Empire.

William Hawkins (1608–11 CE)

- He was dispatched as an ambassador by King James I of Britain to Emperor Jahangir's Mughal palace.

- In 1609, Captain William Hawkins led the inaugural journey of the English EIC to India.
- Despite his efforts, he was unsuccessful in securing Jahangir's approval to establish a factory.

Thomas Coryat (1612–17 CE)

- He was an English traveller during the reign of Jahangir.
- Coryat undertook his journey on foot, departing England in 1612 and arriving in India via Greece, Turkey and Persia in 1615.
- Notably, his description of Italian customs and manners introduced England to the use of the table fork.

Pal Canning (1615–25 CE)

- He was an English tourist who visited during the reign of Jahangir.

Sir Thomas Roe (1615–19 CE)

- He was an ambassador representing King James I of England.
- He visited India during the reign of Jahangir, following the unsuccessful mission of William Hawkins.
- He arrived in Surat with the aim of securing protection for an English factory.
- His work, *The Embassy of Sir Thomas Roe to the Court of the Great Mughal*, stands as a priceless addition to Indian history.

Edward Terry (1616 CE)

- He served as the chaplain for the English embassy during Thomas Roe's visit to India in the durbar of Jahangir.

- He provided detailed descriptions of the social behaviour of Indians in Gujarat.
- He documented his travel experiences in *A Voyage to East-India.*

Pietra Della Velle (1622–60 CE)

- He was an Italian traveller during the reign of Jahangir.
- He authored various accounts detailing his observations about life in India.

Francisco Pelsaert (1620–27 CE)

- He was an employee of the Dutch EIC and commander of the Batavia.
- He resided in Agra and actively engaged in trade.
- He provided a detailed account of the thriving trade in Surat, Ahmadabad, Broach, Cambay, Lahore, Multan and other cities.

John Fryer (1650–1733 CE)

- He was an English traveller and surgeon in the EIC.
- He authored *A New Account of East-India and Persia*, providing vivid descriptions of Surat, Bombay and southern India.

Peter Mundy (1628–34 CE)

- He was a British traveller during the reign of the Mughal Emperor Shah Jahan in 1628.
- He provided valuable insights into the Mughal Empire and the standard of living of common people.
- His records mention being served 'chaa' or tea by the Chinese.

Johan Albrecht de Mandelslo (1638 CE)

- He was a German traveller who wrote about his journeys through Persia and India.

Jean-Baptiste Tavernier (1638–63 CE)

- He was a French traveller and diamond trader.
- He visited India six times during the reigns of Shah Jahan and Aurangzeb.
- He transported the 112-carat Hope diamond to France.

Niccolao Manucci (1653–1708 CE)

- He was an Italian traveller who initially served at Dara Shikoh's court before becoming a doctor.
- He wrote detailed accounts of life during the time of Aurangzeb.

Francois Bernier (1656–1717 CE)

- He was a philosopher and physician hailing from France.
- He visited India during the reign of Shah Jahan.
- He enjoyed the patronage of Daneshmand Khan, a noble under Aurangzeb.
- He authored *Travels in the Mughal Empire,* which discusses the rules of Dara Shikoh and Aurangzeb.

Jean de Thevenot (1666 CE)

- He was a French traveller.
- He described cities such as Ahmadabad, Cambay, Aurangabad and Golconda.
- During his thirteen-month stay in India during the Mughal era, he travelled from Golconda to Masulipatam and then returned by land to Surat to depart for Persia.

Gemelli Careri (1695 CE)

- He was an Italian traveller who arrived at Daman.
- He noted observations on the military formation and administration of the Mughal emperor.
- He realized the potential for profitable trade, particularly in items such as 'dates, wine, spirits, and all the fruits of Persia at Bandar-Abbas on the Persian Gulf, which one carries to India either dried or pickled in vinegar, on which one makes a good profit'[1], to finance his journey.
- His travels inspired the famous book, *Around the World in Eighty Days*.

4

Niccolao Manucci

'The most sumptuous of European courts cannot compare in richness and magnificence with the lustre beheld in Indian courts.'

—Manucci

Niccolao Manucci, often referred to as the Marco Polo of India, was an Italian (Venetian) writer, self-taught physician, diplomat and traveller who wrote firsthand accounts of the Mughal rule. His work, *Storia Do Mogor*, is widely regarded as one of the most authentic sources documenting the events that transpired in India during the Mughal Empire. Manucci resided in India during a pivotal moment in history, as Mughal power was waning and Europeans were establishing their presence. He meticulously documented various folk beliefs, lifestyles and customs of the period with integrity.

At the age of fourteen, hailing from a humble background, he fled his home in Venice without a clear purpose, making his way toward the port. An English vessel bound for Smyrna, Turkey, had already started its departure preparations. As the boarding process neared completion, the boy dashed towards the ship and hastily embarked, never to return to his former life.

The crew, assuming the boy to be the son of a passenger, ignored him. Despite successfully concealing himself in a storeroom for an entire day, hunger eventually forced Manucci to reveal himself to the captain. By then, the ship had already set sail upon the high seas. Surprised by the unexpected passenger, the captain handed him over to an English gentleman named Mr Bellomont, who himself was running away from the British government following a bitter dispute. Bellomont and Manucci deboarded at a port in Turkey, from where they joined a caravan bound for Persia, a journey spanning over a thousand kilometres. Subsequently, they once again boarded a ship, this time heading for Surat.

En route from Turkey to Persia, Manucci was robbed of all his belongings after several unsuccessful attempts, as was often the case in medieval societies. He duly noted in his memoirs that Muslims harassed travellers and occasionally subjected them to violence, sometimes just for amusement. If anyone retaliated, they risked severe consequences, such as having their limbs severed and being forcefully converted to Islam. Women in those regions always covered their faces. Turks also disapproved of non-Muslims wearing green clothing, as the colour was believed to be reserved for Muslims, being favoured and endorsed by their prophet, Mahomed.[1]

Manucci finally landed in Surat in 1655. One of the initial observations that struck him upon his arrival was the Indians' chewing habit: 'Almost everybody was spitting something red as blood.' He assumed it might be due to a tropical disease or perhaps broken teeth. Then, an English lady explained that it was the result of chewing betel leaf (paan). She offered him a paan, and upon eating it, he felt dizzy and nearly lost consciousness. She reassured him that this was a common reaction the first time and that subsequent experiences would be enjoyable. Manucci later observed that it was customary in India to offer paan to visitors. Another aspect that struck him was the open, smiling faces of

Hindu women, contrasting with veiled women in burqas he had seen in Persia and Turkey.

Manucci observed that Surat was a thriving cosmopolitan city even at that time, with trade ships from several countries arriving and departing at the port seeking business. He was intrigued to find people of every nationality engaged in trade, including Europeans, Central Asians, Persians, Armenians and even Africans, many of whom had adopted the country as their new home. He was also surprised by the diversity of religions. He was fascinated to learn about Parsis, who were similar to Hindus in many ways but distinct, being fire-worshippers and wearing a sacred thread.

Despite the Industrial Revolution already underway in Europe, which made it increasingly wealthy, colonialism and enterprise were the main drivers behind the newfound abundance. However, he found Surat to be wealthier than any European city. The accumulated revenue used to flow to the Mughal emperor Shah Jahan's daughter, who would splurge on her own whims and fancies, regardless of the fate of the common people.[2]

Manucci and Bellomont stayed in Surat for seventy-five days, mainly because they could not find a caravan heading towards Agra. Travel was risky due to highways bandits, forcing people to travel in groups. Once, while shooting a peacock in the jungle, Manucci became separated from the caravan. Suddenly, two robbers armed with bows and arrows emerged from behind the bushes and started pursuing him. Although Manucci mounted his horse and galloped, the robbers were gaining ground rapidly.

When he felt escape was impossible, he turned and aimed his gun at them, causing them to flee instead.[3]

Manucci also describes sarais, accommodation for travellers, akin to hotels:

Portrait of Niccolao Manucci, National Library of France, Cabinet of Prints, Paris. Niccolao Manucci is depicted wearing Islamic attire, consisting of striped pyjamas and a kurta, with a waist belt that barely conceals his stomach. His stride seems hurried and unsteady as he carries shrubbery, likely for medicinal purposes.[4]

Journey of Manucci from Venice to India, 1653–55.[5]

For the use of wayfarers there are throughout the realms of the Mogul on every route many 'sarai' (sarde). They are like fortified places with their bastions and strong [gates]; most of them are built of stone or of brick. In every one is an official whose duty it is to close the gates at the going down of the sun. After he has shut the gates, he calls out that everyone must look after his belongings, picket his horses by their fore and hind legs.... At six o'clock in the morning, before opening the gates, the watchman gives three warnings to the travellers, crying in a loud voice that everyone must look after his own things. After these warnings, if anyone suspects that any of his property is missing, the doors are not opened until the lost thing is found, by this means they make sure of having the thief, and he is strung up opposite the sarde. Thus the thieves, when they hear a complaint made, drop the goods somewhere, so as not to be discovered.[6]

Later, Manucci journeyed towards Burhanpur, now in Madhya Pradesh, hoping to meet Aurangzeb with the intention of serving under him. However, Manucci was unable to meet Aurangzeb, as the latter had already departed to Aurangabad to confront rebel Hindus attempting to reclaim their territory. Manucci observed that despite India being under Mughal rule, Hindus frequently launched guerrilla raids in Mughal territories to regain lost land, leading to regular skirmishes between the two communities.

First Contact with Dara Shikoh

Disappointed at not meeting the Mughal prince in Burhanpur, Manucci set off towards Agra via Gwalior. Along the way, in the town of Hodal near Agra, his benefactor Bellomont succumbed to the intense June heat, leaving Manucci orphaned in this unfamiliar world. Eight days later, two Englishmen, Thomas Roch and Reuben Smith, who served as artillerymen in the court of Shah Jahan, approached him disguised in Muslim attire. They demanded that Manucci hand over Bellomont's property, claiming Roch was a relative. They forcibly abducted Manucci and transported him to Delhi over three days, subjecting him to constant verbal abuse, leaving him bewildered by the inexplicable rude behaviour of his fellow Europeans. Upon arrival, they deposited both Manucci's and Bellomont's belongings in a serai outside Delhi, adamantly refusing to reveal their identities despite Manucci's repeated requests. Though he pleaded for the return of his property, they declined rudely. Manucci stayed in another room in the same serai in Delhi, hoping to reclaim his belongings.

Talented though he was, luck often favoured him, and he soon found himself in the company of Clodio Malier, a Frenchman serving as an artilleryman with Dara Shikoh, the eldest son of the Mughal emperor Shah Jahan. Malier informed Manucci that Roch had falsely petitioned Dara, claiming to be Bellomont's relative and seeking possession of his property. When Smith, Roch's accomplice, learned of this scheme, he demanded a share of the spoils. Upon hearing the whole story, Manucci decided to lodge a complaint with Wazir Khan, the king's secretary.

Manucci's personality impressed the secretary, who promptly escorted him to King Shah Jahan. The king sat cross-legged upon his renowned peacock throne (Takht-e-Taus), positioned on a raised platform adorned with golden railings embedded with precious diamonds and gems. His crown boasted the world's largest diamond, the Kohinoor. It was no wonder he was called the richest man on earth, with his wealth estimated at 25 per cent of the world's GDP. Prince Dara sat a few feet below the throne, keenly observing the European newcomer and his confidence in this foreign land. Despite the crowded court hall, a profound silence and order prevailed, maintained by vigilant security officials to prevent any disturbance that might displease the king. After submitting his petition to the king, Manucci returned filled with hope. The next morning, he was escorted to Wazir Khan's residence, where all his and Bellomont's belongings were kept. In a corner stood two Englishmen, shackled in iron chains. After speaking his mind for a few minutes, Manucci chose to forgive them.

Accompanied by Malier, Manucci paid a visit to Dara Shikoh, Aurangzeb's elder brother, who was contending for the throne. For some inexplicable reasons, Dara showed favouritism towards Europeans. Another advantage Manucci possessed was his working knowledge of Persian, which was the court and intellectual language of Mughal India at that time. Manucci had acquired knowledge of Persian and the understanding of the delicate court etiquette of Muslims during his travels from Turkey to the Persian port. He later reflected on this episode in his memoirs:

> When I left Venice I already knew sufficiently how to speak the Italian language, and in addition a little French. During this journey I learnt the Turkish and Persian languages. Finding myself established in India, I now set to work to learn the Indian tongue. Furthermore, as I was desirous of knowing about matters in the Mogul kingdom, I found an aged man of letters, who offered to read to me the 'Royal Chronicles of the Mogul kings and princes'.[7]

He proved himself to be an eager learner of the skills necessary for day-to-day survival in India. He also seemed to have acquired a practical knowledge of Urdu, the vernacular language of common Muslims.

Urdu was an amalgamation of Persian with old Hindi. Sufi scholar Amir Khusrau started the literary tradition of Urdu in the 14th century, but it gained prominence among the Mughals only during Aurangzeb's reign. The name Urdu originated from the Turkic word ordu (army), denoting the 'language of the (army) camp'. Muslims, however, were reluctant to adopt an Indian script, as everything associated with India was considered inferior to Arabic and Persian. Hence, they opted for Nastaliq, an obscure Persian script, to assert their superiority. Nevertheless, its grammar was rooted in Sanskrit and classified as part of the Indo-Aryan language family. Despite this, it predominantly remained the language of Muslims, whom the British derisively referred to as 'Moors'. John Ovington, an English missionary and contemporary of Manucci, wrote in 1689:

> The language of the Moors is different from that of the ancient original inhabitants of India but is obliged to these Gentiles for its characters. For though the Moors dialect is peculiar to themselves, yet it is destitute of Letters to express it; and therefore, in all their Writings in their Mother Tongue, they borrow their letters from the Heathens, or from the Persians, or other Nations.[8]

Even after four or five centuries, it remained exclusively the language of Muslims, and currently, only 4 per cent of Indians speak it. However, in northern and western India, it is prominently displayed on government signboards and Hindi film posters to highlight the country's secularism.

Impressed by the young European, Dara hired him for the princely sum of Rs 80 a month. Manucci felt indebted to him, but he had a sixth sense that everyone in India wanted to convert him to Islam. He started taking extra precautions regarding this. He was also surprised to discover that there were many Europeans in India, even within the Mughal court, and few of them had converted to Islam. Most were surgeons, with the remainder being artillerymen. Even at that time, Europeans held the esteemed position of top artillerymen, responsible solely for aiming, while the rest of the laborious tasks such as raising, lowering, loading and firing were delegated to locals, primarily Hindus.

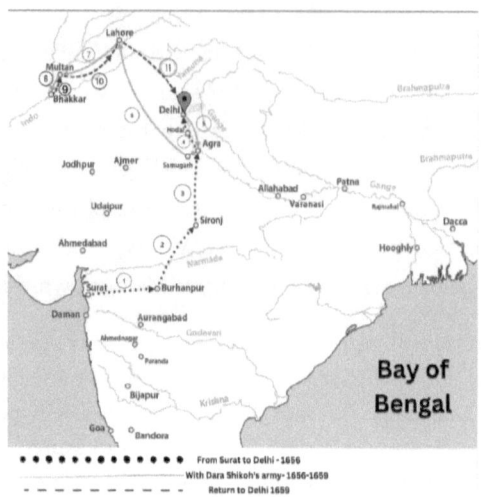

Inland Journey of Manucci in India, 1656–59.[9]

Succession Battle

As destiny propelled Manucci to an enviable position in the Mughal prince's court, he became an eyewitness to all the intrigues of the royals. He witnessed how every Mughal prince harboured intentions of eliminating their father, brothers and other relatives. Although Shah Jahan, as frail as he was, delegated all his powers to Dara, his younger brothers – Shah Shuja, Murad Bakhsh and Aurangzeb – were unable to accept it. This was primarily because Dara was not deemed suitable for the Sultanate, being more inclined towards poetry and otherworldly pleasures. He showed little interest in maintaining his army, but when Aurangzeb challenged him to battle, he was compelled to hastily assemble one. Due to paucity of time, he could only assemble a ragtag bunch such as butchers, barbers, blacksmiths, carpenters, tailors, etc. Very few trained soldiers were enlisted, rendering his army no match for the seasoned and experienced soldiers of Aurangzeb. The outcome of the battle that ensued in May 1658 at Samugarh, near Agra, was already evident to many.

Despite knowing he was on the losing side, Manucci served as an artilleryman alongside Dara in the battle.

Amidst the tension of the succession between the Mughal princes, one Champat Rai Bundela played a significant role. He was an ambitious king of Bundelkhand who engaged in guerrilla warfare against Shah Jahan. The Mughal emperor, however, disapproved of these skirmishes and suppressed the revolt. Bundela, aware of Shah Jahan's fondness for Dara, sought revenge. When Aurangzeb prepared for battle against Dara, he needed to traverse Bundela's territory to cross the river via a lesser-known fjord, located approximately 36 miles away, in order to surprise Dara. Aurangzeb sent valuable presents and promised Bundela high rewards in the future. These demands were promptly accepted by Champat, who harboured a strong desire to see Dara defeated. However, he did not anticipate Aurangzeb's treachery. The day before the battle, after crossing the river, Aurangzeb summoned Champat to his tent under false pretences and summarily beheaded him.

This drawing illustrates the key moment during the Battle of Samugarh in 1658 when Dara Shikoh, after his howdah was struck by a rocket, dismounted from his elephant to continue fighting on horseback. Upon seeing the empty howdah, his troops mistakenly believed that Dara Shikoh had been killed and began to retreat. On the right side of the picture, Aurangzeb can be seen in his howdah, while at the bottom right, Murad Bakhsh is seen fleeing the battlefield.[10]

On the battleground, Dara Shikoh inexplicably dismounted from his elephant, which promptly fled from the chaos of the fighting. The fleeing elephant served as confirmation for Dara's troops, leading them to mistakenly believe that their leader had been killed. Almost immediately, his entire troop fled. Manucci noted that the Mughals lagged behind the Europeans by several decades in terms of equipment and strategy. He particularly highlighted the tendency to retreat from the battlefield if the leader fell. Europeans, on the contrary, had well-defined succession plans in battle, which foreshadowed their eventual dominance on the world stage.

Realizing his mistake, Dara fled from Agra to Delhi and then to Lahore. His subsequent stops included Multan, followed by Bhakkar (Thatta) in Sindh, with Manucci accompanying him throughout the escape. Meanwhile, Aurangzeb captured Agra Fort and overthrew the Mughal emperor Shah Jahan, who was in poor health, on 8 June 1658. Immediately afterward, Aurangzeb, leading his army, relentlessly pursued Dara, considering him a significant threat. Dara then journeyed from Sindh to Kathiawar, where he encounter Shah Nawaz Khan, the governor of Gujarat, who provided him access to his treasury and assisted him in recruiting a new army. Nevertheless, Dara remained apprehensive of his younger yet ruthless brother's formidable forces. Simultaneously, he grew weary of constantly evading capture and seeking assistance from influential figures. His last hope lay in receiving support from his friend and powerful Marwar Rajput king, Jaswant Singh. However, losing confidence in Jaswant, Dara redirected towards Ajmer and resolved to confront the relentless pursuers dispatched by Aurangzeb.

On the other hand, Jaswant Singh, like numerous other Rajput kings, faced his own set of challenges. He was not an all-powerful king but rather acted upon the directives of Shah Jahan. His responsibility was to oversee the Mughal princes and prevent them from reaching Agra. His army consisted of a disparate collection of Rajput clans with minimal coordination. He found himself in a profound dilemma as he was reluctant to take sides. Noted historian Jadunath Sarkar explains his predicament:

> At all times, a subject opposing two princes of the blood, a servant fighting for a distant master against two chiefs who acknowledge no higher authority than their own will, is severely handicapped. In Jaswant's case the natural inferiority of his position was aggravated by the commands he had received from Shah Jahan.[11]

On 11 March 1659, Dara fought against Aurangzeb in the battle of Deorai in a do-or-die struggle but suffered a devastating defeat and sought to escape to Persia to save his life. Despite opposition from his family, he set out for Persia and reached Bolan Pass (now in the Baluchistan province of Pakistan at the Afghanistan border), where his first wife Nadira died due to dysentery. Death was swiftly catching up with him too.

Sketch by James Atkinson (1842), showcasing the entrance to Bolan Pass, Balochistan, Pakistan.[12]

Since it was hot at that time, he feared that the majority of his troops might perish in the treacherous mountain pass. Abandoning his plan to travel to Persia, he moved to Sindh and sought asylum with Malik Jeevan (Junaid Khan Barozai), an Afghan tribal lord whose life Dara had saved from Shah Jahan's wrath on multiple occasions. Dara thought he would find protection in exchange for his assistance. Malik Jeevan, however, did not hesitate to arrest his benefactor at the first opportunity. He proudly informed Aurangzeb that he had captured Dara Shikoh. Aurangzeb immediately dispatched his army, and on 10 June 1659, Aurangzeb's army captured the most-wanted brother in Mughal history.

Aftermath of Dara's Death

Manucci did not accompany Dara on this journey, as the prince asked him to return to Delhi. He later wrote in his memoirs that Dara Shikoh was eventually brought to Delhi, chained, made to sit on a dirty elephant and paraded through the capital's streets. Aurangzeb could have killed his brother then and there, but since Dara was a popular prince, he did not want to risk civil unrest, and so he had to follow due process of justice. He called his chosen mullahs (Islamic religious teachers), who declared Dara an apostate of Islam.

Dara was exploring the convergence of milder interpretations of Islam and the Upanishads and had written a seminal work, *Majma ul Bahrain* (*The Mingling of the Two Oceans*), considered blasphemous by the Muslims. He had been introduced to Vedantic philosophy by a Udasi mystic, Lai Dass. He also believed that the Upanishads were 'without doubt or suspicion, the first of all heavenly books in point of time, the source of the fountain of reality and ocean of monotheism, in conformity with the Holy Quran and even a commentary thereon'.[13]

A few years earlier, he had heard about Sarmad Kashani, an Armenian Jew who had translated the Torah into Persian. India was prosperous, and upon learning that valuable goods and artwork were being purchased in India for exorbitant prices, Sarmad packed up his belongings and set out to sell them in the Mughal Empire. Arriving in Sindh, he began observing life there.

Earlier, Dara heard about him and was impressed with his work, even inviting him to his father's court in 1654. However, interacting with a Jew was strictly forbidden for a pious Muslim. Due to these activities, Aurangzeb would later brand Dara an infidel. In the dead of night on 9 September 1659, Dara was hacked to death by Aurangzeb's henchmen in front of his terrified son, and his head was severed in a cruel Islamic manner.[14]

However, the story did not end there and had a more gruesome conclusion. Aurangzeb thoroughly examined the severed head to confirm its identity as Dara's. He then inflicted three additional wounds on the head with his sword. Following that, he ordered that the head be placed in a box and delivered to his ailing father, Shah Jahan, with explicit instructions that it only be given to him during his dinner in prison. The guards were instructed to convey, 'King Aurangzeb, your son, sends this gift to let you see that he does not forget you.' Shah Jahan was initially overjoyed and exclaimed, 'Blessed be Allah that my son still remembers me.'[15] However, upon opening the box, he was shocked and immediately fainted. Dara Shikoh's remains were later interred in an unidentified grave within Humayun's tomb in Delhi.

After receiving his reward for loyalty from Aurangzeb, Malik Jeevan and his fourteen nobles were stoned to death near Sirhand (Sar-i-hind, the Frontier of Hind, as the Mughal emperors considered it the 'gateway to Hindustan', now in Punjab).

As mentioned earlier, the world over, any new Muslim sultan used to eliminate all contenders for the throne. In this pursuit, familial ties held no weight; fathers, brothers and even sons were not spared. Following this well-established philosophy, Aurangzeb seized the first opportunity to kill his brother Murad Bakhsh, while he forced Shah Shuja, another brother, to flee to Burma, solidifying his position as the undisputed shehanshah.

Manucci, however, had remained loyal to Dara throughout, and Aurangzeb was well aware of this. He, along with other Europeans, was arrested and presented before the new king, who offered him double pay to serve the court. Politely declining, as he refused to work under his master's murderer, Manucci was surprisingly released respectfully by Aurangzeb. Perhaps, Muslims held white men in high regard and treated them with deference.

Later, Hazrat Sarmad Shaheed was summoned to Aurangzeb's court in 1661 to be questioned about his association with Dara and certain accusations of blasphemy. Sarmad, like Dara, explored Hinduism and attempted to integrate and teach its virtues. He observed multiple instances of nudity in Hinduism and Jainism, and admired the spiritual attainment by Naga Sadhus and Digambar Jains upon renouncing worldly affairs.

Sarmad had previously been in a homosexual relationship with a Hindu boy named Abhay Chand. When rumours started circulating, the boy's parents removed him from Sarmad's company, prompting Sarmad to became distraught and commence walking around naked. Since then, he adamantly refused to wear any clothing, as Manucci noted, he would rather lose his head than wear clothes. Like garments, he quickly outgrew the need for religion too. He later came to be known as the 'Jewish Saint of India' or 'Jewish-Yogi-Sufi Courtier of the Mughals'.

Aurangzeb had encountered Sarmad previously, in 1655, when he was still a prince. Once, while passing through a street, the prince found Sarmad sitting naked in a corner. Upon questioning, the naked ascetic requested that Aurangzeb cover him. Aurangzeb obliged, only to find the nearby blanket concealing the severed heads of those murdered by the prince. Sarmad then pointedly asked Aurangzeb what should be covered: his nakedness or the prince's sins?

Manucci had encountered him several times in Dara's durbar but remained unimpressed by his nudity, considering it uncouth, uncivilized and barbaric.

Aurangzeb receiving Dara Shikoh's head.[16]

In the Mughal court, Sarmad laughed at Aurangzeb and rebuked him for causing so much suffering, including Dara's demise. Aurangzeb questioned Sarmad about why he only repeated, 'There is no God', and ordered him to recite the complete phrase, 'but Allah'. Sarmad replied, 'I am still absorbed with the negative part. Why should I tell a lie?'

Enraged by his defiance, Aurangzeb ordered his immediate execution, his '*sar tan se juda* farman', which was immediately carried out. Muslims have historically been swift in carrying out beheadings.

Sarmad's grave is located near the Jama Masjid in Delhi. Many speculate that he was killed because of his homosexuality and nudity, but this is far from the truth. Every Muslim sultan of significance kept several male sex slaves, especially when female slaves were not available, such as during the desolate nights of battles. Many sadhus freely roamed the countryside naked without drawing attention. Sarmad was primarily punished for his friendship with Dara. Later, Maulana Abul Kalam Azad remarked, 'Sarmad's crime was that he drank the cup in public, while others drank in private.'[17]

Naked Shah Sarmad seated with Dara.[18]

Manucci's friendship with Dara was legendary, and he supported the prince through thick and thin. In contrast, he harboured an equal dislike for Aurangzeb. This antipathy may have stemmed from Aurangzeb's religious fanaticism compared to Dara's open-mindedness. Dara also liked Manucci for his quick wit, fluency in Persian and unwavering loyalty. Dara commissioned the translation of the Upanishads, which was later taken to Europe by Francois Bernier, a contemporary of Manucci. Impressed by the unique and profound thought within, a French linguist named Abraham Hyacinthe Anquetil-Duperron translated it into Latin. The German philosopher Arthur Schopenhauer became a Hinduism enthusiast after reading this translation of the Upanishads. In this way, Dara's contribution to disseminating Hindu knowledge in Europe was substantial, although it is often overlooked. With Dara's death, India missed a new dawn after five centuries of subjugation. If Dara Shikoh had ascended to the throne, India would have been a very different nation.

The Role of Dancing Girls in Indian History

During his extensive travels all over India, Manucci repeatedly encountered the challenges of Indian life in general and of the Mughals in particular. Whenever he stayed in the *sarais* or hotels, he was pestered by various salesmen peddling goods and services of all kinds. He also observed the presence of another kind of trade, the oldest profession in the world, which seemed to thrive without shortage of women of pleasure in India.

As a close friend of Dara and later a doctor, he had insights into the intrigues of imperial courts, royal harems and grand zenanas. The harems were always bustling with dancing girls, as they were expected to provide heightened pleasure to their masters.

He observed that Mughal princes were notorious for their obsession with 'dancing girls'. These were typically young girls and women, mostly Hindus, who were fully exploited and discarded once their usefulness waned. Prince Salim (Jahangir) had Anarkali, while Aurangzeb himself had Heerabai by his side. Baz Bahadur, the Muslim ruler of Malwa, took Rupmati, a beautiful dancing girl, into his harem in Ujjain. However, when Mughal prince Akbar learned of her beauty, he sought to possess her at any cost. He marched on Malwa to claim her, but upon arrival, he discovered that Rupmati had taken her own life by drinking poison.

Jahandar Shah, grandson of Aurangzeb, engaged in another scandalous affair with Lal Kunwar, a descendant of the renowned musician Tan Sen and a beautiful dancing and singing girl known as the Singing Empress. He bestowed upon her the title of Imtiaz Mahal (the chosen one of the palace). Although she was unmarried, she was granted the imperial insignia and an annual stipend of Rs 2 crore, an unimaginable sum in those times.

Mohammad Shah 'Rangila', another Mughal king, was perhaps the most infamous of them all. He was known, first, for his singular preoccupation with sex and, second, for his scandalous liaisons with Nur Bai, a courtesan. Both were frequently spotted together in public places. Nur Bai was often described as 'bulbul ki awaz, hoor ka sarafa' (having the voice of a nightingale and the appearance of an angel). Queen Qudsia Begum considered her a formidable rival and always feared that one day Nur Bai would surpass her.

The queen's fear was not unfounded. Nur Bai had already expressed her desire to become a queen one night after she glimpsed the Kohinoor concealed in Mohammed Shah's turban. However, Shah rudely rejected her advances. Since then, she had been waiting for a chance for revenge, biding her time. Fate presented her with an opportunity sooner than expected when Nadir Shah attacked Delhi in 1738. Recognizing the roving eyes of the Persian invader, she seized the God-sent opportunity. That night, while spending 'quality' time with Nadir Shah, she divulged the secret of the Kohinoor, which held great value to Mohammed Shah. Normally, Nadir Shah kept his hand on his sword, but this time, he opted for a more tactful approach. He requested an elaborate farewell from the Mughal king on the eve of his departure for Persia.

In the ceremony, Nadir Shah proposed the exchange of turbans, citing it as a Persian tradition. Mohammed Shah's expression soured, knowing he could not refuse due to Nadir's reputation for tyranny. Soon, the Kohinoor found its way to Persia, along with its 'sister', the Darya Nur, and a vast treasure including '700 elephants, 4,000 camels, and 12,000 horses carrying wagons all laden with gold, silver, precious stones and the magnificent Peacock Throne', valued at an estimated £87.5 million in today's currency.[19]

Nur's legacy will be remembered for changing the course of Indian history, unlike the many thousands of other dancing girls who lived and died merely to satisfy the cruel whims of their Mughal oppressors. Nur herself faced brutal torture before her eventual, albeit slow, death.

Like all Mughals, Dara Shikoh too fell in love with a lowly dancing girl named Rana-dil, demonstrating his somewhat non-conformist approach even in matters of love. However, this did not mean Dara had no other wives; he had two more, Nadira and Udaipuri Mahal, an Armenian whom he had married before his affair with Rana-dil began.

Unfortunately, like other dancing girls, Rana-dil too didn't meet the Mughal standards according to Dara's 'abbu jaan', Shah Jahan. Only after Dara threatened suicide did Shah Jahan consent to their marriage. However, compared to other kings and princes, Dara had the fewest wives. For instance, Akbar was rumoured to have 300 wives, while Jahangir had as many as 20.

Rana-dil, however, remained loyal to Dara. After his death, Aurangzeb sought to add her to his vast harem. When she learned that the king admired her gorgeous black hair, she cut it off and sent it to Aurangzeb, expressing her desire to live alone. However, Aurangzeb did not take rejection lightly. So infatuated was he with her beauty that he offered Rana-dil all the honours and rights of a queen. Upon hearing this, she slashed her face with a knife, collected the blood and sent it to the king, saying that if he desired her beauty, it was now gone, and if her blood satisfied him, he was welcome.

This story is far from a typical Valentine's Day tale. It recounts a unique love affair involving a prince now remembered solely for his fanaticism, violent nature and apparent lack of affection. It is the story of Aurangzeb experiencing love at first sight, and even he could not resist the charm of the dancing girls. In 1636, he became deeply enamoured with Heerabai, one of the dancing women in his harem, and his intense affection for her led him to neglect his prayers and austerities for a while. She was a Kashmiri Hindu who, in her childhood, was sold in the slave market and came into the possession of Mir Khalil, a governor of Khandesh province. When Aurangzeb saw her, he fell in love with her and asked for her from his governor, who resisted initially but later agreed, however, only on the condition of bartering her with another girl in Aurangzeb's harem. She was given the surname Zainabadi Mahal because, ever since the reign of Emperor Akbar, it had been decreed that the names of the women in the imperial harem should not be publicly mentioned. Instead, they were to be designated by an epithet derived from their place of birth or the city or country where they had entered the imperial harem.

Aurangzeb spent his days immersed in music and dance, and even indulged in wine at the urging of the dancer. When she died, Aurangzeb vowed never to drink wine again or listen to music. Later in life, he often remarked that Allah had shown him great mercy by ending the dancer's life, as she had led him into numerous sins and almost cost him the throne due to his indulgence in such vices.

Manucci's writings reveal that dancing girls, known as *tawaifs* or nautch girls, held a unique and respected place in Indian society. These women were not merely entertainers; they were accomplished artists trained in classical music and dance and often highly educated. They performed in the courts of the Mughal emperors and regional Hindu kings, where they played a significant role in cultural and social events. Their performances were not just about entertainment but were also seen as a sophisticated art form, showcasing intricate dance movements and expressive storytelling through their graceful gestures and facial expressions.

However, Manucci also noted the duality in their status. While they were revered for their artistic talents, they were also seen as courtesans and were often associated with prostitution. This association with prostitution did not necessarily carry the same stigma as in contemporary Western societies; rather, it was an accepted part of the social fabric. The *tawaifs* were often courted by noblemen and royals and could wield considerable influence in court politics and social circles.

Prostitutes, on the other hand, occupied a different stratum. According to Manucci, the lives of these women were marked by hardship and exploitation. Unlike the *tawaifs*, they lacked social standing and artistic respect. Many were forced into prostitution due to poverty or were sold into the trade at a young age. Their lives were perilous, with little protection from abuse and disease. Despite their marginalized status, prostitutes were a visible and integral part of urban life in the 17th century, serving the needs of both local men and foreign travellers. However, prostitution has existed since time immemorial worldwide, and it would be wrong to single out medieval India.

Manucci's observations also highlight the intersection of power, gender and economics in the lives of these women. The *tawaifs* and prostitutes were both subject to the desires and whims of powerful men, yet they navigated their circumstances with resilience and agency. The *tawaifs* leveraged their talents and connections to secure patronage and influence, while prostitutes, though more vulnerable, found ways to survive in a harsh and often unforgiving environment. Many of these dancing girls rose through the ranks to reach the top, as Manucci vividly describes in his books.

Dance, Music and Literature in Indic Civilizations

While the dancing girls of the Mughal era represented sexual exploitation and abuse, historically, dance and music in the Indic civilization had served as a means not only to worship the divine but also to depict the ancient epics.

Indian classical dance, along with music and literature, traces its origins back to the Natya Shastra, an ancient Sanskrit text on the performing arts compiled by Bharat Muni between 200 BCE and 200 CE. This text describes the Tandava dance of Lord Shiva from which all other Indic dances originate.

Although the dances varied by region across the land, all forms were unified in providing spiritual and cultural fulfilment. Styles included Bharatanatyam, Kathak, Kathakali, Kuchipudi, Manipuri, Mohiniyattam, Odissi and Sattriya. When combined with music, these dances offered a beautiful theatrical experience for all and served as a powerful means of transmitting the ancient epics of the scriptures and historical stories to the masses. Performances would take places in the inner sanctum of temples, royal palaces and public places such as fairgrounds and schools.

However, invasions by the Mughals and later the Europeans made the indigenous sacred art of dance less accessible to the masses. Instead, Hindus became accustomed to the sexualized dances that had initially originated in the harems and brothels of their oppressors. In the land where once women and men had danced to worship their gods or celebrate their warriors, they were now compelled to dance to satisfy the wanton desires of their intoxicated invaders. The impact of this is still evident centuries later in contemporary Bharat, where Bollywood movies often showcase salsa, disco, belly dancing and even pole dancing, with classical forms like Bharatanatyam and Kathak notably absent.

Manucci did not write about the classical dances of India, as he probably never got a chance to see them in Mughal India. It was during his travels in the British and French regions of present-day Tamil Nadu that Manucci had the opportunity to witness classical dances. In his miniature painting book, *Libro Nero*, there were two illustrations depicting south Indian ritual dancers, out of a total of sixty-six illustrations.

Manucci's Love for Dara, Warts and All

Manucci remained deeply impressed by his former master, Dara, and expressed:

> The first-born son of King Shahjahan was the prince Dara, a man of dignified manners, of a comely countenance, joyous and polite in conversation, ready and gracious of speech, of most extraordinary liberality, kindly and compassionate.... Dara was very fond of Europeans. Added to this, as everyone knew, he held to no religion. When with Mahomedans, he praised the tenets of Muhammad; when with Jews, the Jewish religion; in the same way, when with Hindus, he praised Hinduism. This is why Aurangzeb styled him Cafar (Kafir) – that is to say, 'The Infidel'.

At the same time he had great delight in talking to the Jesuit fathers
on religion, and making them dispute with his learned Mahomedans,
or with a Hebrew called Cermad (Sarmad), an atheist much liked by
the prince.[20]

Manucci, nevertheless, was also aware of Dara's flaws, particularly
his arrogance as a learned Mughal. He wrote, Dara was 'over-
confident in his opinion of himself, considering himself
competent in all things and having no need of advisers'.[21] Dara
despised those who offered him advice. Thus, his closest friends
refrained from informing him about crucial matters necessary to
survive in the challenging world of Muslims.

Opting not to serve Aurangzeb proved to be a prudent
decision on Manucci's part as he started showing his fanatical
tendencies and imposed numerous cumbersome restrictions
on Hindus. Christians, despite being considered people of
the book, 'ahl-e-kitab', were also forcibly converted. Many
of Manucci's European friends converted voluntarily after
observing the prevailing trend. Hindus faced even harsher
treatment, being barred from riding horses, elephants or
palanquins. While Holi and Diwali were allowed, they came
with unbearable limitations. Several temples, including the
Somnath and Kashi Vishwanath Temples, were destroyed
and converted into mosques. Aurangzeb also banned the
construction of new temples and the repair of existing ones.
Additionally, they were prohibited from wearing fine clothing.
It was a feared Sharia law, offering no means of escape.

Manucci Goes for a Career Change

After his master's death, Manucci realized that he was back to
square one, without anyone in his life. At just twenty-one years
old, he was fed up with all the warfare in India and was seeking
a change in his job profile. However, unsure of what to do, he

decided to stay in Delhi for a few years. Fortunately, destiny smiled upon him and presented him with a promising opportunity.

European physicians began arriving in India from the 16th century onward, employed by European trading companies. Trained in contemporary European medical practices, they attended to the medical needs of company soldiers and officials. Many other Europeans also possessed rudimentary medical knowledge to handle tropical diseases and emergencies. As a result, every European came to be regarded as a doctor and held in high esteem. Another Italian, Bernardino Maffei, had previously served as the chief surgeon of Shah Jahan.

One day, an Uzbek chieftain living in Manucci's neighbourhood in Delhi fell severely ill. Manucci was immediately called for a diagnosis and medication. Despite being a school dropout, his curiosity once again led him to the patient's house. There, he assumed the role of a doctor, wearing a grave expression and muttering some medical jargon. Although he could not diagnose the illness, he was eager to uphold his reputation, so he returned under the pretext of preparing the medicine. Without delay, he sought out his Portuguese friend Joao de Souza, who had some rudimentary medical knowledge. While Joao suggested some medication, the patient showed no improvement even after three days. During one visit to the patient's home while the family was having dinner, Manucci observed that they were consuming spoiled meat in an unsanitary room. He reprimanded them for their unclean eating habits and lack of proper etiquette. Manucci prescribed fresh Uzbek food, and lo and behold, the patient indeed began to recover in the next few days. Since then, he never looked back.

His initial medical case seemed more like a performance than genuine treatment. Even so, word quickly spread in the streets of Lahore that 'a Frank doctor had arrived, a man of fine manners, eloquent speech, and a great experience'.[22]

Though excited by his newfound status as a 'doctor', he also feared repercussions, so he always left some disclaimer to maintain his reputation. In Delhi, he lived with Jesuit priests to study medical science. He sent a gold ring back home with instructions for it to be sold for books on medicine, which were to be sent back to him. After several questionable attempts as a medical practitioner, he did manage to cure some influential patients. With these successes, he seemed to secure some work as a physician in the court of the Mughals.

Later, he settled in Agra, where he encountered another European, a Dutchman named Jacob, who had fled the Portuguese atrocities in Goa and had knowledge about medicine. One day, a Mughal royal summoned Manucci to treat a fistula, a task no one else was willing to undertake. Despite the reluctance of others, Manucci, accompanied by the fugitive Dutchman, accepted the challenge and successfully cured the royal within a few days. He continued his avid study of medicine, and soon his fame spread widely, earning him a place on the committee of surgeons in the Mughal court.

Subsequently, he relocated to Lahore, seeking a degree of anonymity. His medical practice flourished to the extent that rumours circulated about a 'firangi' doctor capable of resuscitating the dead. His 'doctory' became so renowned that he came to be known as Hakim Manucci. It's likely his inspiration to pursue medicine stemmed from his fellow European, Francois Bernier, a French physician who arrived in India in 1658 and became the chief physician of Dara Shikoh.

During his medical career, Manucci faced a blasphemy charge, a grave accusation carrying a certain death penalty. Thika Arain, a ferocious bandit who plundered Mughal territory, was eventually captured and publicly executed in accordance with Islamic tradition. Knowing of his impending execution, Manucci saw an opportunity to obtain human fat for his homemade ointments for skin diseases and injuries. He directly petitioned Fidai Khan, the governor of Lahore, for the fat of the bandit. Surprisingly, his request was swiftly granted, and he acquired 504 ounces from the deceased. Manucci successfully produced an ointment from it, which he claimed to be highly effective.

However, during this episode, there was a qazi who was quite jealous of him and also angry because he was being bypassed by Manucci. He spread a rumour that Manucci took the fat of a devout Muslim and was now using it to treat other Muslims. Meanwhile, the governor was transferred, and now the qazi had free rein. He complained to the emperor enthusiastically in the hope of having Manucci executed. But to his horror, the king dismissed the case by stating, *'Qazaya-i-zamin bar-sar-i-zamin.'*[23] *('Cases about land are settled on the land itself.')*

An assassination attempt soon followed. One of Arain's nephews came to avenge the corpse's dishonour in the guise of a patient. However, upon witnessing Manucci's sincere treatment of his patients and the beneficial use of his uncle's fat in aiding humanity, he changed his mind. He spared Manucci and departed after confessing his true intentions, contrary to the typical Indian tradition, without even accepting paan from Manucci.

The qazi, however, was made of steel. His ego was wounded multiple times, all thanks to Manucci, a 'lowly firangi'. He sent someone to coax Manucci and extract the secret of oral medication using human fat. However, Manucci detected the deception and asserted that it was solely for skin application. After conceding defeat, the qazi later confessed to Manucci that he himself had consumed human fat multiple times, but in secrecy.

Journey to Bengal

In due course, Manucci once again grew weary of his sedentary life. In 1662, he set out towards Bengal to explore the eastern region. He enlisted the help of two Portuguese men, fleeing from the tyranny of their countrymen carrying out the Inquisition, as his servants for this new journey. He spent a considerable amount of time in Allahabad and observed how Hindus bathe in the Ganga to purify themselves. He noted that despite losing family members and friends in stampedes during the numerous melas, Hindus do not mourn; instead, they rejoiced that the deceased have attained moksha in the holy city.

After enjoying the natural beauty of the city for a few days, he proceeded to Banares, another ancient city. He documented that a few years after his visit, Aurangzeb ordered the demolition of all temples in the area. Manucci also learned that fine Banares textiles with gold and silver embroidery were highly sought after and exported worldwide.

Continuing his journey, he arrived in Patna, where he found both Dutch and British factories, producing and exporting fine-quality silk, clay artefacts and saltpetre. After spending some time there, he travelled to Calcutta, where he encountered British, French and Dutch factories once again. He kept meeting Europeans throughout India, feeling a sense of belonging during these encounters. From Calcutta, he proceeded to Rajmahal, near Qasim Bazar (now in Jharkhand).

In Rajmahal, he encountered a large crowd and learned of a tragic incident. A married Hindu woman was involved in an extramarital affair with a musician. Together, they meticulously planned and killed her husband. However, the musician refused to marry her as they had previously agreed. According to Bengal custom, the woman was now forced to commit sati. Before her death, she was expected to donate her jewellery to her loved ones.

The musician's greed led him to the site to claim his share. Upon seeing him, tears welled up in her eyes. She handed him one of her necklaces, embraced him tightly and jumped into the raging fire. Before she could be rescued, the fire had already claimed her life.

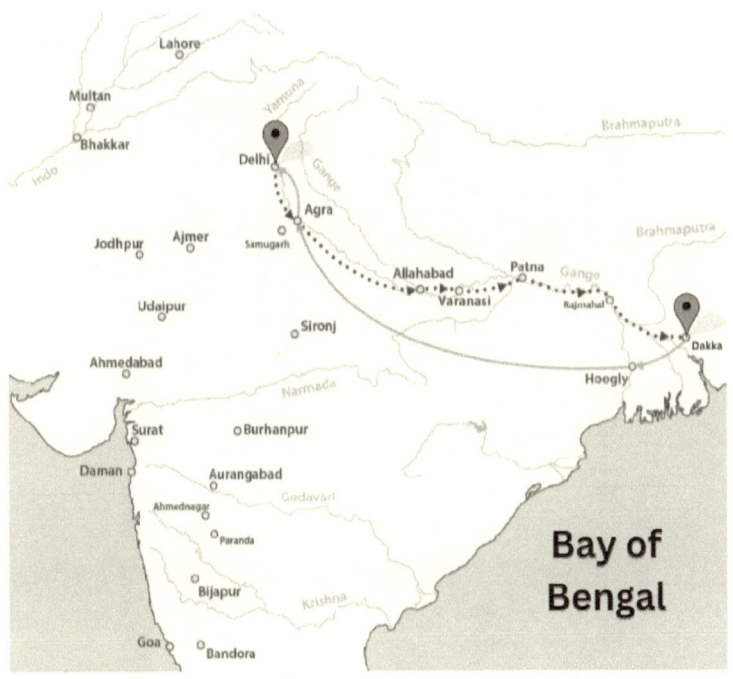

The Journey of Manucci from Delhi to Bengal in India, 1662–63.[24]

According to Manucci, on his way back to Delhi from Bengal, he witnessed the governor of Bengal, Shaista Khan, sending Bengal's revenue to the Mughal king in the form of three hundred cartloads of silver and fifty cartloads of gold coins, heavily guarded. Manucci also stated that Bengal's share amounted to a whopping Rs 4 crore in 1663, which surged to Rs 5 crore 50 thousand in 1707.

In 1663, upon returning to Agra after several months, Manucci encountered another woman being coerced into committing sati.

Manucci sought assistance from his Christian Armenian friend to rescue her. The Armenian agreed, and both unsheathed their swords, entering the crowd with a battle cry. The sight of the swords caused many to flee, and the Armenian lifted the woman onto his horse and escaped. Later, he facilitated her conversion to Christianity, married her and settled in Surat.

Miniature painting of a woman performing sati by Niccolao Manucci.[25]

Brush with Sorcery

During this period, Manucci forged a friendship with the Rajput king, Jai Singh, having served under him for some time. Singh was now in the employ of Aurangzeb, who harboured a strong rivalry with Shivaji. Singh might have been the only Hindu in whom Aurangzeb placed such great trust that he was referred to as 'Mirza' Jai Singh. It was no surprise that Aurangzeb selected Singh to lead the Deccan expedition against Shivaji. Manucci himself accompanied them on this venture. However, Singh later fell out of favour when Shivaji managed to escape from the Agra Fort. Singh and his son Ram Singh were blamed for the fiasco, and as punishment, Ram Singh was sent to Assam to fight lengthy battles with the Ahom king.

Jai Singh tasked Manucci with a mission to visit the three Hindu rajas of Ramnagar, Pent and Chottia, respectively, and persuade them not to support Shivaji. As security, he was required to bring back their sons. Jai Singh compensated Manucci handsomely for this assignment, an offer he could not refuse. Initially, Manucci visited Ramnagar and, through a combination of promises and threats, persuaded the king to offer his son as collateral. He then proceeded to Pent and obtained the king's son as a guarantee. Unfortunately, the son of the Pent king succumbed to sunstroke during the journey.

Accompanied by his entourage and the captive son of the kingdom of Ramnagar, Manucci went to the third king. Although initially reluctant, the king agreed after Manucci threatened him with dire consequences. Since the king had no son, he offered his brother as collateral. During his stay, the king developed a fondness for Manucci's horse, a gift from Jai Singh. He offered Rs 1,000 for the horse, but Manucci refused. However, when misfortune befell the horse and it lost its legs in an accident, the king persisted in his offer, prompting Manucci to suspect sorcery. Then, the king increased the price to Rs 1,200, but, this time the offer lacked politeness. Sensing a shift in the situation, Manucci quickly agreed to sell the horse.

Leaving with his caravan, which had grown quite large with all the gifts, he proceeded to Agra. On the way, they passed through a radish field, and his servant attempted to pluck a juicy one. Somehow, his hand became entangled in the branches and could not be freed. The landowner had to be summoned, and after bribing him, he murmured some mantras, and lo and behold, the branches retracted, and the servant was released. Since then, Manucci held a strong belief that Indians were quite proficient in witchcraft.

Manucci recounted stories of witchcraft in detail, where women were said to control their lovers. The young men would become infatuated with these women, sometimes to the point of insanity. Manucci knew of men who refused to marry or be with other women in case their lovers died prematurely. In another instance, a woman struggled to conceive despite consulting many doctors. As a last resort, she sought out a magician who instructed her to stand naked under a banyan tree in a deep forest at midnight and perform certain spells. The woman did conceive a child after nine months, but the tree never bore fruit and remained barren throughout its life. However, in another unfortunate case, a magician exploited a woman desperate to conceive.

Manucci criticized Hinduism for the superstitions prevalent in India and proudly proclaimed that such incidents did not occur among Christians, who followed the 'true faith'. To his dismay, even Christians began to fall victims to such spells. In 17th-century Portuguese-ruled Chennai, a Christian man fell in love with his maid. His friends attributed it to a magical charm cast by the lady, as he showed no interest in anyone else. Even when visitors came to his home, he only wanted to talk about her. Once, he fell seriously ill with diarrhoea, yet remained preoccupied with her. When his friends learned of his condition, they severely beat the maid and demanded her she lift the spell. Afterwards, he could not even bear to look at her. It remained uncertain whether it was truly a spell.

In another instance, a Portuguese man living with his family fell in love with his Hindu servant girl. It fuelled the girl's ambition to become the lady of the house after eliminating her lover's wife. She approached a magician, who instructed her to gather nail clippings, hair and some clothing belonging to her landlady. With these items, he fashioned a doll and asked her to take it to the garden of the house at midnight, stark naked, and burn it. The burning doll was then to be placed beneath her mistress's bed. However she failed to complete this task out of fear, resulting in her landlady fainting and falling ill with a fever instead of dying. The partially burnt doll was discovered three days later, and another magician was summoned to remove the spell with considerable effort. It still took the mistress over three months to recover. The servant girl was subsequently dismissed and later found begging on the streets.

Manucci recounted another incident involving a rich Portuguese man in erstwhile Madras who fell in love with a Hindu girl from his neighbourhood. He sent her a romantic letter in an inappropriate language, which the girl gave to her mother. The mother consulted a magician, who suggested some charms and spells. The man would often linger in front of her house to catch a glimpse of her. The next day, when he approached the girl's door, he was first denied entry but was later allowed in, only to be coerced into marrying her on the spot. A Brahmin was called, the marriage was solemnized and the girl went to live with him. However, he became suspicious and imposed severe conditions on her freedom. The girl contacted the magician again, who provided her with magical oil, which she rubbed on the sole of her husband. With her husband under her spell, she started meeting her lover in his absence. When the girl's younger sister learned of the elder sister's enjoyment, she too moved in with her lover. Both sisters led carefree lives while the husband, under the influence of magic, remained unaware. However, their scheme was uncovered one day when the elder sister witnessed a Christian procession from her window, causing her to faint. Chaos ensued, and their lovers were apprehended, leading to the sisters being executed by the Portuguese authorities. Afterwards, their parental home became haunted, and everyone who dared to stay there met an untimely demise.

Manucci recounted yet another incident involving the unattractive brother of the Mughal governor, Shaista Khan, who had become the subject of ridicule after Maratha king Shivaji daringly cut his fingers in a guerilla attack in Pune. The brother's repulsive appearance made him reluctant to go out, so Khan sought the help of a magician in Agra. During Manucci's visit to him, the magician performed a seemingly miraculous act, causing fruits like peaches, pears and apples to appear out of thin air, even though it was not their season. Although the brother offered him these fruits, Manucci declined, knowing they were tainted.

Many Europeans who arrived in India during the medieval era believed in stories of witchcraft just as the Indians did. Witchcraft was even employed to intimidate the Mughal army in Assam by Ahom commander Lachit Borphukan. Sorcery and witchcraft continue to be feared in the eastern parts of India, especially in Bengal and Assam. During my time in Assam, it was believed that needles or nails were not sold after sunset, as shopkeepers feared buyers might use them for hypnotic or harmful purposes. These items were seen as potent conduits for magical mantras, and thus, many ancient civilizations buried nails and hairs as a precautionary measure.

A Chance Meeting with Shivaji

One night in 1664, after meeting Jai Singh, the entourage camped, and Shivaji came to meet the prince. There he encountered Manucci, and both were suitably impressed with each other. Manucci noted that Shivaji's soldiers were far more brave and rugged than those of the Mughal army. Shivaji's strategies were also superior, as he did not hesitate to relinquish a fort now and then in pursuit of greater gains in the future. Manucci proceeded to enlighten him about the battle technology, tactics and strategies of European nations. In line with the custom of Muslims and Christians, he also extolled the virtues of his religion, perhaps harbouring a faint hope of converting him.

Niccolao Manucci in a Mughal costume.[26]

Mughal Harems

Manucci spent almost his entire life in India and witnessed both the admirable and abhorrent aspects of the land, from the depraved to the holy, the cruel to the benevolent. He served as a privileged observer of India's rich history and cultural diversity. His book, *Storia Do Mogor*, detailed these facets of Indian life, chronicling the reigns of Mughal kings such as Shah Jahan and Aurangzeb and princes like Dara Shikoh, Shah Alam and Rajput king Jai Singh. He extensively detailed Mughal depravity, depicting how sons fought against fathers and brothers fought amongst themselves for power, with no quarter given in this ruthless game. New, more brutal methods of torture were devised daily to subdue enemies, regardless of their Hindu or Muslim identity. His underlying narrative suggests that Muslims were characterized by their reliance on sex and swords.

Manucci was astounded by the sexual appetite of Muslims and the splendour of Mughal harems. According to him, the Mughal mindset required harems filled with multitudes of women, often numbering in the thousands. Muslims held a special affection for women and found solace in their company. Typically, each harem housed around 2,000 women of various races, whose main purpose was to provide sexual pleasure to the king. After being 'sampled' by the king, the women were either distributed amongst relatives and friends or sold in the slave market.

Every harem followed a standardized architecture, with each room assigned to a courtesan or wife. There were no doors, allowing the sultan unrestricted access. Entrance for the king was normally located in the centre, allowing him to move freely wherever his desires led. The room layout was devised to conceal the king's movements, ensuring that no one could know his whereabouts. As the saying goes, he was akin to a gamecock, reigning supreme over all.

However, the harem served purposes beyond mere sexual pleasure, as it also served as a place for raising children and housed facilities such as hammams, kitchens, schools and playgrounds. Furthermore, royal treasures, secret documents and royal seals were also stored in the harem, including the Kohinoor, which was once housed in the harem of Delhi Sultan Ibrahim Lodi.

According to Manucci, the women in the harem lived a luxurious lifestyle, albeit devoid of freedom or rights. Every morning, new clothes arrived for the royal women, and previously worn garments were never reused but instead distributed to the slaves. The royal ladies would often recline naked near the fountains during the day and enjoy fireworks at night. They entertained themselves with activities like chicken fighting, listening to ghazals, engaging in archery and hearing stories, all of which were integral parts of their daily lives. Those who excelled in these pursuits were elevated to higher ranks within the harem hierarchy and sometimes involved in political affairs. Other women, relegated to the harem's periphery, sought to satisfy their sexual desires through alternative means, including interactions with doctors like Manucci, who encountered many such incidents, which he described in detail.

Another custom in the Mughal harem was that when a doctor attended to a female, his face remained covered throughout the visit. Shah Alam abolished such customs as an additional incentive to retain Manucci, arguing that Christians had purer minds compared to Muslims, 'The minds of the Christians were not filthy like those of the Mahomedans.'[27]

This unexpected opportunity enabled Manucci to observe the harem up close, quite literally. Once, a royal woman feigned illness, prompting his visit for a checkup. There was a purdah separating the doctor and the patient, with a hole for the hand to feel the pulse. The woman took his hand and placed it on her chest. Manucci managed to maintain a straight face, lest the eunuch standing just behind them catch on. He recounted:

[When] the physician stretched his hand inside the curtain where the woman lay, she would 'lay hold of it, kiss it, and softly bite it. Some, out of curiosity, apply it to their breast, which has happened to me several times; but I pretended not to notice, in order to conceal what was passing from the matrons and eunuchs then present, and not arouse their suspicions'.[28]

Manucci further stated:

[The] king took it into his head to fix the costume of the women in his harem, dividing them into groups or companies—that is, so many got up in such a manner and such colours, another company in another colour, and so on for the whole of them. He was also anxious that these clothes should all be of the finest materials procurable.[29]

Manucci also mentioned that the king built a special hall for the greater satisfaction of his desires. It was twenty cubits long and eight cubits wide, adored throughout with large mirrors. It consumed a huge amount of money, with the gold alone costing Rs 1.5 crore, not including the enamel work and precious stones, for which no account was kept. He believed that all this expenditure was made so that he might obscenely observe himself and his favourite women.[30]

Muslim women were exempted from the burqa only in their harems or homes. Outside, they had to wear the all-black veil, regardless of how hot it was. Manucci recalled that Muslims were in the habit of smoking incessantly. Taking advantage of this addiction, every sultan levied a heavy tobacco tax to increase revenue for the royal treasury. This led to smuggling, and to curb it, tax inspectors were appointed at the entrance of every city. Once, a Muslim soldier and his family were travelling to Delhi in a covered vehicle, and an inspector stopped him, wanting to search the vehicle for tobacco. The soldier replied that his wife was inside and he dared not search. The inspector, hoping for a major haul of illegal tobacco, did not listen, uncovered the vehicle, and tried to enter it. Losing his temper, the soldier drew his sword, cut the inspector's head, and injured many of his assistants. Not content, he went on to kill his wife and daughter. He was overpowered and presented to Aurangzeb, who was impressed with the soldier for following Sharia rules. He was released without punishment. The tobacco tax was abolished, causing sadness among inspectors and merchants alike.

Like other travellers, Manucci was also interested in how normal Indian women behaved. He could write about women, especially those of the harem variety, accurately because of his unique abilities. He was a doctor, with white skin, confident and had a good knowledge of Persian, qualities highly valued by women of the era. This combination was indeed rare, and he mostly enjoyed the power it afforded him.

Manucci also wrote about devadasis, the temple dancers:

> The facts of which I speak are very well known throughout India, and many mothers, by reason of some danger or necessity, or difficult delivery, offer to the temple the virginity of their female infants.... In addition, there are public women, dancers, who are required to appear several times a week to sing and dance before the idol. For this purpose, they have some allowances, from which they are under obligation not to be absent.[31]

A Full-Fledged Doctor

Manucci kept longing to live with his European counterparts from time to time and went to Vasai, near Mumbai, in 1666. The Portuguese were carrying out the Inquisition and executing heathens at will. In this regard, they were no less brutal than Muslims. Manucci was also deemed insufficiently Christian and faced punishment, prompting his escape to Goa sometime in 1667. However, the weather did not suit him, and he desired to leave as soon as possible.

Once again, he found himself on the road after securing his safety and reaching Aurangabad. There, he received news that Prince Shah Alam, Aurangzeb's son, was in hot pursuit of Shivaji. Manucci was asked to aid in this expedition, but he had no desire to involve himself again in the incessant warfare in India. He departed for Agra, then Delhi, and finally Lahore in late 1667. Over the next ten years, his medical practice thrived until 1676 when he became entangled with Muhammad Amin Khan, the governor of the city and viceroy of the Lahore province. Khan wanted Manucci's service, but he refused. Khan did not take his refusal lightly and forcibly took him to Kabul. However, Manucci managed to escape en route and sought refuge with his old friend Mahabat Khan, who provided him with protection.

However, Mahabat had fallen out of favour with Aurangzeb, who was determined to eliminate him through poisoning. Manucci was strictly instructed not to provide any medical assistance to Khan under any circumstances. One day, Manucci sent him some homemade wine, but halfway through, a spy tampered with the bottle and poisoned the wine. As a result, Mahabat fell ill, and he began to suspect Manucci of collusion with Aurangzeb. In an effort to prove his innocence, Manucci drank from the same bottle, demonstrating that the wine was not poisoned. After remaining unharmed for several hours, Mahabat was reassured of Manucci's loyalty. However, despite Manucci's efforts, Mahabat succumbed to the effects of continuous, slow poisoning a few days later.

As a keen observer, Manucci also noted some peculiar Muslim customs. One day, he witnessed an Uzbek slashing the neck of a horse with a sharp knife, causing the blood to gush out like a

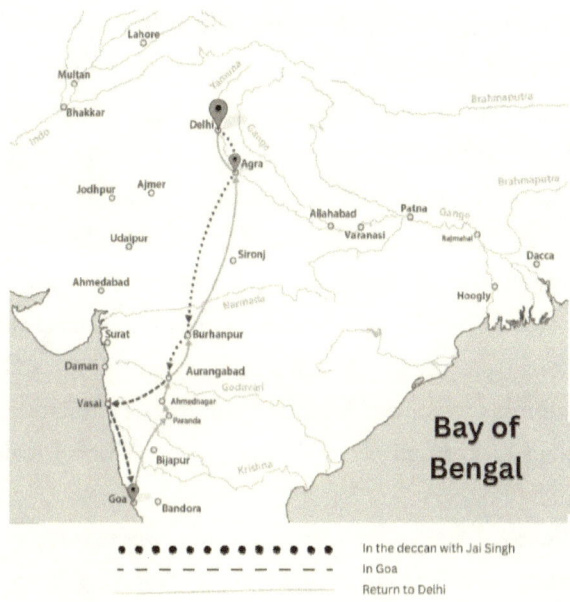

The Journey of Manucci from Delhi to Goa, 1664–67.[32]

fountain. The Uzbek immediately started drinking from the flowing blood, and soon, other Muslims joined in, lapping up the blood like wolves. Shockingly, before the horse succumbed to its injuries, the wound was stitched up, prolonging its suffering until death. When Manucci inquired about this barbaric act, they proudly stated that it was their tradition to leave nothing alive in enemy territory, whether it be humans or animals.

After some time, Manucci once again took up employment as the personal physician of Prince Shah Alam in Agra. Impressed with his medical skills, the prince and his wife sought to retain him for life, knowing Manucci's slippery persona. They proposed that he marry one of their maids in the harem, offering him a choice of European, Armenian or any other nationality as well as any religion – be it Hindu, Sikh, Christian or Muslim. Manucci saw through their scheme and declined, even pretending to be impotent. However, the prince's wife remained unconvinced.

Later, Alam suggested that Manucci convert to Islam to gain further benefits from the Mughal court. Manucci, resolute in his beliefs, refused, citing his allegiance to Christianity. Unwilling to accept defeat to a 'lowly firangi', Alam persisted in his efforts. One day, a rich girl arrived at Manucci's house seeking refuge. Despite her beauty and fine jewellery, he turned her away, suspecting another one of Alam's tricks. Shortly after, another girl and her elderly maid sought shelter with him, offering material concessions from the court. Once again, Manucci refused, wary of any attempts to convert him, having heard of similar deceitful conversions of Portuguese individuals in the Mughal realm not long ago.

As a doctor, Manucci's favourite method was to bleed patients by puncturing the veins in their arms, believing it to be an

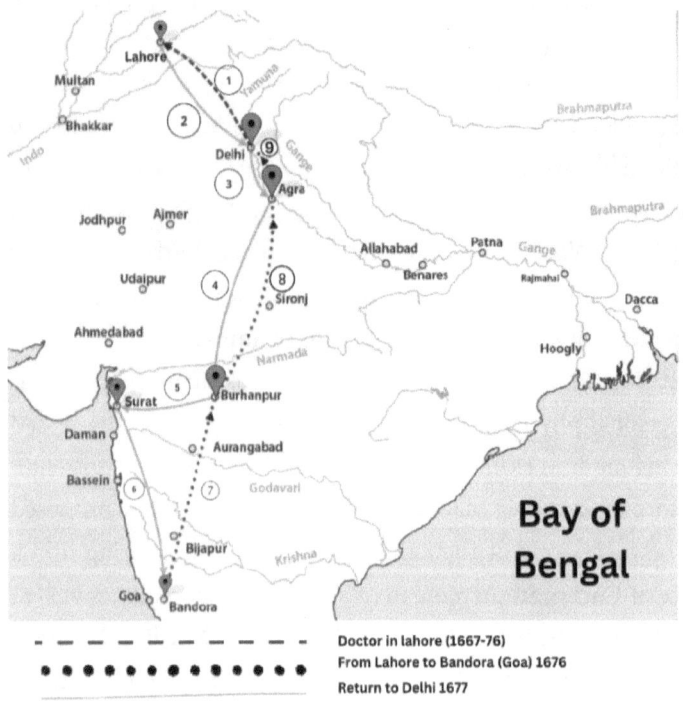

Doctor in lahore (1667-76)
From Lahore to Bandora (Goa) 1676
Return to Delhi 1677

The Journey of Manucci from Delhi to Lahore via Surat, 1667–77.[33]

effective cure. Despite his success, envy from Hindu and Muslim doctors led to rumours that he drank the blood of Muslims after bleeding them. Curiously, the rumour did not mention Hindus, reflecting their marginalized status where their lives were less valued. To dispel this rumour, Manucci started donating blood in the evenings and warned people that they would turn into animals if any creature, such as a cat or dog, consumed it.

During his time in India, Manucci faced numerous assassination attempts, primarily by Europeans possibly driven by jealousy of his reputation and wealth. Fortunately, luck often favoured him, allowing him to escape unharmed, albeit narrowly.

Once, a rich Muslim widow fell in love with him and was willing to sell all her possessions to flee to Europe with him. They made elaborate plans together and even met frequently at his house. However, a loose-lipped Portuguese friend revealed their intentions, leading to threats from another suitor of the widow. Eventually, she married this suitor but was murdered just eight days later. Manucci, rather than feeling any romantic attachment, was just concerned that a Muslim woman had potentially been forcibly converted to Christianity.

Growing tired of the politics at the Mughal court, Manucci requested leave from Shah Alam to attend personal matters in Surat. After spending a few months there, he journeyed to Goa.

Aurangzeb: Destructor-in-Chief

After Shivaji's death in 1680, his son Sambhaji became Aurangzeb's primary enemy. Aurangzeb aimed to besiege Goa, intending to use it as a strategic base against the Marathas. When Mughal forces led by Prince Shah Alam advanced towards Goa, the Portuguese viceroy, realizing his army was no match for the Mughals, sought someone to negotiate with him. He turned to

Manucci for meditation, and the negotiations proved successful. The agreement allowed the Mughals unhindered passage through Portuguese territories to attack Sambhaji, with a pledge not to harm anyone in Goa. For his exemplary services, Manucci was awarded with the Knight of the Order of Santiago by the Portuguese, enhancing his fame and wealth.

However, he could not maintain good relations with the Portuguese for long and had to flee Goa, disguised as a monk, heading to Bijapur, a Maratha territory. The road was infested with thugs and robbers who had a penchant for murdering travellers. He passed several *chungis*, checkpoints where money was collected from travellers. The extortion imposed on travellers was severe, depriving them of even the smallest amounts of money. The thugs showed no compassion for the poor, taking their shirts, coats or any other possessions if they lacked money.

Upon reaching the holy city of Pandharpur, a rumour spread that he was carrying several precious pearls. A group of robbers attacked him at night, but since the doors were closed, they could not harm him, and he had to flee for his safety. While running helter-skelter for his life, he noticed an open door of a house and took shelter on the roof. The landlord realized that his house had been intruded upon and soon appeared with a sword in his hand, forcing him to leave. He sought refuge in a temple but was dismayed to find a large crowd had already assembled there after escaping from the mayhem in the streets.

From there, he fled to the bazaar and took shelter in another shop. This time he was lucky, and after spending a rather uncomfortable night, he crossed the Bhima River and reached Aurangabad, a Mughal city. He learned a lot on this journey and observed that travelling taught him many things. He reflected that anyone who wandered without learning anything could be likened to having the mind of a fool.

During Manucci's stay in India, Aurangzeb remained his arch-nemesis. Manucci, however, was quite aware of the emperor's power and fanaticism and kept a safe distance from him. He wrote in detail how much the Mughal emperor hated Hindus and issued frequent orders to destroy Hindu temples:

> The latter [Aurangzeb], rid of a rajah [Raja Jai Singh] whose influence might have been dangerous to his kingdom, declared that very hour an open war against Hinduism.
>
> He sent orders at once for the destruction of the fine temple called Lalta, in the neighbourhood of Dihli. He also ordered every viceroy and governor to destroy all the temples within his jurisdiction.[34]

He also wrote about how Aurangzeb destroyed the temple at Mathura and renamed it Islamabad.

> Among others was destroyed the great temple of Matora (Mathura), which was of such a height that its gilded pinnacle could be seen from Agrah, eighteen leagues away. In its place a mosque was to be erected, to which he gave the name of Essalamabad (Islamabad)—that is, 'Built by the faithful.' Not content with this, he expelled the jogis or sanydsls, who are the ascetics and saints of the Hindus.
>
> He directed that the higher officers at the court who were Hindus should no longer hold their charges, but into their places Mahomedans should be put. He hindered the Hindus from enjoying their merry-making (intrude) or carnival, (Holi) on which occasion Mahomedans also resort to pranks and filthy sports.[35]

However, during his extended stay in India, Manucci befriended only Muslims and Christians, considering Hindus irreligious and heathen, and, as Abrahamic are fond of saying, without any faith. In all his books, he rarely praised Hindus. He also bemoaned the fact that no one in India observed Catholic practices. About Holi, he stated the following:

The time of this festival or carnival falls ordinarily on the moon of March. It is their custom to disport themselves by throwing on each other's clothes scented oils and odoriferous dust, if they are personages of position, or dirty water and other stinking things if they are low people. They run about in all directions, just as with us in Europe is done at carnival time, with noisy cries and obscene words.[36]

Contrary to his reputation, Aurangzeb often showed no mercy to fellow Muslims as well for minor transgressions. In 1687, Aurangzeb displeased with the Golconda sultans, swiftly laid siege to Golconda Fort in Hyderabad. By September 1687, a traitor had opened the eastern gates, allowing Mughal forces to breach the fort and capture Governor Abul Hasan. Aurangzeb's cruelty knew no bounds; Hasan was imprisoned in the fortress of Daulatabad and tortured until his death. The Mughals plundered over Rs 6 crore in gold and silver coins from the fort, reducing the Qutb Shahi Sultans to mere commanders and administrators within the Mughal army. Manucci, present in Golconda at that time, wisely chose to flee the siege, seeking safety in the Portuguese territory of Madras.

Finally Settled in Madras

Manucci eventually settled in Madras on St Thomas Mount (or Parangi Malai, 'foreigner's hill'), but he kept alternating between the cities of Pondicherry, Arcot and Madras. He established a good working relationship with the English EIC, acting as their intermediary with the Nawab of Arcot. However, he longed to return to his motherland.

During a visit to his friend Francois Martin, governor of Pondicherry, Manucci was advised not to return to Europe and instead to marry a suitable Christian girl in India itself. He was introduced to Elizabeth, a Catholic widow, whom he married in 1686. They had a son, but sadly, he died in infancy.

Throughout his stay in India, he maintained good relations with the powers-to-be, whether it was the Mughals, Portuguese or British. He was in an excellent friendship with Thomas Pitt, the English president of Madras, who later became famous for looting a 410-carat diamond mined from Kollur mines in Golconda. Later, the diamond came to be called the Pitt diamond, surpassing all diamonds known in the world in beauty and weight at that time. It was found by a slave in 1698, who hid it in a wound in his left leg. However, a British captain discovered it and took possession after killing the slave.

The captain sold it to a prominent Indian diamond merchant, Jamchand, for a hefty amount. In 1701, it was bought by Thomas Pitt for £20,400 and sent to London after he concealed it in his son's shoe in 1702. After news of the theft spread, Pitt was mocked. Unfazed by the ridicule, Pitt had the diamond cut to only 141 carats by the diamond cutter Harris to enhance its brilliance. He later sold it to the French royals for an astounding £135,000 in 1717, roughly seven times its purchase value. Like Britain, France was thriving at that time due to colonial gains, and they could afford to buy it. Since then, it has remained in France and is now displayed in the Louvre Museum in Paris. Its current value is estimated at an astonishing Rs 500 crore. Its flawless brilliance and perfect cut affirm its status as the finest diamond in the world.[37]

Manucci Writes a Book

Manucci later resumed his practice as a physician and, in his spare time, started writing. He became even more wealthy and built two palatial houses, the second one in Pondicherry.

It took almost fifteen long years for him to complete the book as he kept juggling between cities, professions and patrons. He could have finished it earlier, but he suffered the loss of his wife, Elizabeth, as well as his close friend, Francois Martin, in quick succession. He included 130 miniatures in his book depicting Indian life, most of which he created himself. These items have been included in the supplements called *Libro Rosso* (Red Book) and *Libro Nero* (Black Book). Both books derive their titles from the colours of their leather covers. The fifty-six miniatures of the Red Book illustrate key characters of Mughal history, durbar, kings, princes and luminaries. The paintings were crafted by Indian artists led by Mir Muhammad, librarian of Muazzam-Shah Alam at Aurangabad. It was sent to Europe in 1701 through André Boureau-Deslandes, a French official working in India. Manucci always took care of his manuscripts, ensuring that they did not fall into the wrong hands.

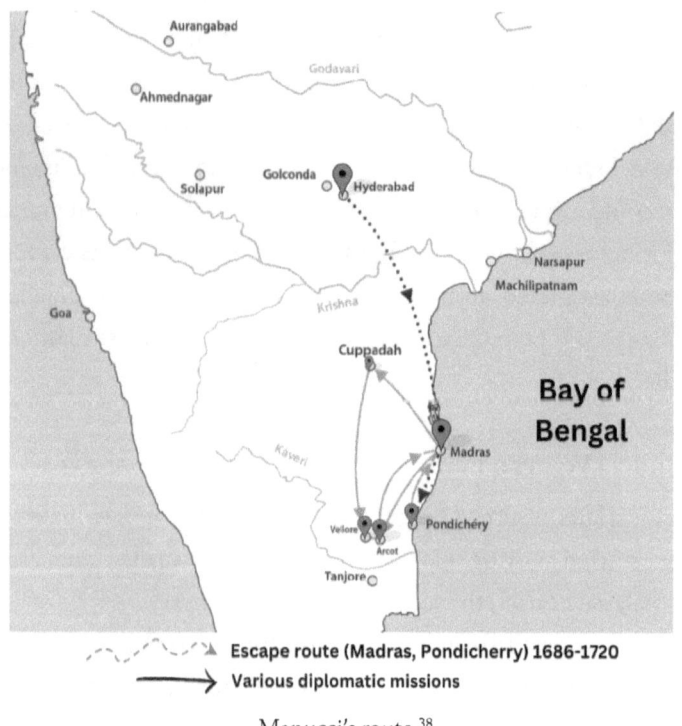

⌁⌁⌁⌁⌁ **Escape route (Madras, Pondicherry) 1686–1720**
⟶ **Various diplomatic missions**

Manucci's route.[38]

The miniatures of the Black Book capture diverse moments of civil, religious and social life among the Hindus of south India; they starkly contrast with the Islamic scenes of the Mughals.

While residing in Madras, Manucci became fascinated by local practices and commissioned native artists to paint them. The Black Book was sent to Europe in 1705, along with books I–IV of the *Storia Do Mogor*, which are now housed in the Biblioteca Nazionale Marciana in Venice. While sending his books, he wrote:

> I send another book with 66 figures which represent the false heathen gods, and how these heathen marry, their burials, penitence, sacrifices, ceremonies, with their significations, as can be seen in the heathen religion, which is treated in the third part.... I believe that my nation, which I greatly esteem, will, after having read my work, be satisfied (as to its authenticity etc.).[39]

Depiction of a processional chariot with devadasi dancers attending to the murthi.[40]

He wrote about his magnum opus, *Storia Da Mogor,* 'I must add, that I have not relied on the knowledge of others; and I have spoken nothing which I have not seen or undergone.'[41]

However, many lies and errors did find their way into the book, inadvertently or not; we may never know. It has not always been feasible to verify his pieces of evidence. Manucci has a tendency to embellish his own adventures, successes and role in the events. Undoubtedly, he held himself in high regard, much like many Europeans, perhaps due to his significant achievements. However, when discussing events in which he was not directly involved, his evidence seems to be quite reliable.

He sent the manuscript of *Storia Do Mogor* to the French historian François Catrou in 1707 for publishing in Europe, but to his unpleasant surprise, Catrou published them as *Histoire générale de l'empire du Mogul* in 1715, claiming authorship. However, karma caught up with him. The Venetian publishing industry, no longer as prosperous as before, could not afford the substantial publication cost, and the book failed to make an impact in the market.

The book's fortune, or one might say Manucci's fortune, took a turn for the better when William Irvine, a British civil servant in India, discovered a copy in Berlin. After translating it into English, he published it under the title of *Storia Do Mogor* or *Mogul India* in four volumes in 1907. The books came to be regarded as a primary source for the study of 17th-century Mughal and Indian history, blending diverse origins and adorned with miniatures by Indian artists.

The main reason for its success was the frankness and honesty with which he wrote about everyone, especially those he served under such as Mughal princes like Dara Shikoh and Shah Alam. In addition to Mughal and Hindu princes, he established connections with the Portuguese and English as well. He was a rare individual who acted as a 'go-between' with different established and emerging power centres. Manucci's artillery work, his book and his Indian experience distinguished him from other European travellers, primarily due to the length of his stay in India.

Conclusion

In the 17th century, Europeans of all kinds were attempting to colonize the world. Vasco de Gama's discovery of India in 1498 is considered a pivotal moment in world history, even by Adam Smith, the renowned economist. Before that, trade between Europe and India had to go through the Arabs and Ottomans. The discovery ended such intermediaries and marked the decline of Islam. Within two centuries, Europe started dominating the globe. The British were already present in India when Manucci was born. He probably saw significant opportunities in the geopolitics of that time. However, why did he suddenly leave home without informing his parents? Was he tired of life at such a young age, or did he yearn to explore the world? We may never know. Niccolao Manucci was intelligent, adventurous and handsome.

He passed away around the year 1717 after spending a remarkable sixty years in India, between 1656 and 1720. No European traveller had stayed in India for such an extended period, as normally, the journeys of 'firangis' to India lasted no more than two or three years. Throughout most of his time, he acted according to circumstances, which made his stories both interesting and genuine. As for the rest, he wrote with keen observation.

His contribution to Indian history is immense, and few could have portrayed India as interestingly as he did. His world included sultans and naked fakirs, doctors and robbers, priests and charlatans, queens and prostitutes, humanity and cruelty, morality and extreme depravity.

No one was infallible in his world.

5

William Hawkins

'An Englishman withouten a stronge drinke is like a fysshe out of water.'
—William Hawkins

Sir William Hawkins, born in 1575, was an English merchant, naval commander and diplomat who played a significant role in the early 17th-century English efforts to establish trade with the Indian subcontinent. He became a key figure in the early interactions between the English EIC and the Mughal Empire.

In 1600, Hawkins set sail for the Indian subcontinent aboard the *Hector*, one of the initial vessels of the newly established English EIC. His early experiences in the area were fraught with challenges, including conflicts with Portuguese forces aiming to retain control over Indian trade routes. Despite these obstacles, Hawkins succeeding in establishing communications with Jahangir, the Mughal emperor, in 1609. His diplomatic acumen and the favourable impression he left on the emperor paved the way for future English engagements in the region.

Hawkins faced considerable challenges from both European rivals and internal dissent within the English EIC. His endeavours faced opposition, and he grappled with competition from Portuguese and Dutch trading interests. Despite the setbacks he encountered during his time in India, his diplomatic achievements established the framework for future English trade and diplomatic relations in the Mughal Empire.

His contributions played a crucial role in shaping the trajectory of English trade and diplomacy in south Asia. Through his early voyages and diplomatic missions, he established the foundation for British rule, which would come to define the history of India during the colonial era.

The Situation in the 15th and 16th Centuries around the World

After the discovery of America and India in the late 15th century, Spain and Portugal reaped astronomical profits from their numerous colonial ventures. Almost all indigenous populations of these continents were decimated, with any survivors forcefully converted to Christianity. Ancient civilizations such as the Aztecs and Incas, thriving for millennia, were obliterated in less than a year. Spain colonized Central and South America within a decade and seized control of the Philippines in the Pacific Ocean in less than a year. On the other hand, the Dutch were reaping significant profits from the Indonesian spice trade. Rumours suggested they were making profits up to 4,000 per cent on a single voyage. Portugal, meanwhile, extended its colonial influence in many parts of South America and even across the vast regions of southern and western India. In this broader context, Britain felt excluded from the seemingly boundless spoils and was eager to secure its fair share.

In 1577, the English explorer Francis Drake, the third person to circumnavigate the globe, embarked on an expedition to the Spanish colonies in South America with the objective of acquiring gold and silver. Sailing across the vast Pacific Ocean aboard his ship *Golden Hind*, he ultimately reached the East Indies and encountered the Moluccas, famously referred to as the

Spice Islands. This venture proved highly lucrative, as enormous quantities of exotic spices were traded for items such as linen, gold and silver. The return on investment for those supporting this expedition was astonishing, exceeding 5,000 per cent.

By the 1520s, the Portuguese were making inroads in India and had started setting up unauthorized trading posts in Bengal. The Mughals reacted strongly to this incursion, launching a swift attack that resulted in the deaths of hundreds of Portuguese. This incident changed the course of Indian history. This episode led the Europeans to realize that the approach taken in North and South America was not applicable to India. They understood that establishing trading posts was the initial step before considering territorial occupation.

Recognizing the challenges and limitations in India, the British concluded that trade rather than violent conquest was a more viable approach. Hence, their traders petitioned Queen Elizabeth I for permission and support to sail to the Indian Ocean. Their intention was to conclusively challenge the Spanish and Portuguese monopolies in overseas trade.

In 1592, the British secured a significant victory over the Portuguese in a pivotal battle, resulting in the capture of the Portuguese vessel *Madre de Deus*, then the largest in the world. The British subsequently transported it to Britain. Along with valuable treasures such as gold, silver and spices, they obtained a particularly precious booklet containing crucial information about China and India.

In 1600, 101 British traders assembled and formed a joint-stock company named the East India Company (EIC), with an investment of £30,133 (equivalent to over £4,000,000 in today's money). They also acquired approval in the form of a royal charter from Queen Elizabeth, a prestigious endorsement at the time, granting them a monopoly on trade with countries in the Indian Ocean. This granted them exclusive rights in the form of monopolies, with the requirement to pay taxes, while monarchs assumed no risks in the expeditions. Flush with funds and armed, British ships began seizing Spanish and Portuguese vessels, quickly amassing profits. Initially, during the first two voyages, British explorers bypassed India, instead targeting rival ships near the islands of Indonesia, where Portugal already had a presence. Britain was hesitant to engage Portugal directly, as it was already embroiled in conflict with Spain and Portugal in Europe. However, it was their third voyage that would alter the course of world history, especially that of India.

During that era, India was firmly under the rule of the Mughals, with Jahangir presiding over its extensive territories. The Portuguese had already held control of the western coast for over a century. To establish a presence and circumvent direct confrontation with the Portuguese in India, the English needed to secure permission from the Mughal Emperor. In 1607, for the third voyage, William Keeling was appointed the captain of a fleet comprising several ships. He was deeply in love with his wife Anne and wanted to be with her all the time, desperate to take her on the voyage.

However, there was a major hitch: at that time, the company's policy dictated that women were not allowed on voyages to the East, out of concern that they might be vulnerable to advances from natives. Keeling persisted by submitting a request to the company, seeking permission for his wife to accompany him on the voyage to India, which the company declined. Undeterred, he clandestinely brought his wife aboard the ship *Red Dragon*. However, in a ship crammed with 200 men, her presence was soon discovered, and she was disembarked at the next port. Three years later, when the ship docked again upon its return, she was undoubtedly there to greet her beloved husband.

From the Horn of Africa, Keeling set off for Bantam in Indonesia, entrusting explorer William Hawkins with the command of the EIC's ship *Hector*. The *Hector*, a small ship accommodating only 100 individuals, was tasked with handling all diplomatic affairs. Hawkins's inclusion in the expedition was primarily due to his proficiency in Turkish and Persian, essential for dealings in Mughal India. However, trading with India posed significant political challenges, as obtaining permissions from the Mughal kings was imperative to establish factories and conduct commerce. Hawkins arrived with letters and gifts from King James for the numerous kings, princes and governors of India.

The expenses for these gifts were relatively modest, but the potential gains were expected to be immense. The human tendency to be drawn to gifts, regardless of one's social status, has long been exploited by astute individuals. Recipient often view such gifts as complimentary, yet there is invariably an underlying cost, often exceeding initial expectations. This phenomenon guided Europeans, who adeptly deciphered the vulnerabilities of indigenous populations worldwide. Emperor Jahangir, in this regard, was no exception.

On 24 August 1608, the *Hector* dropped anchor off Surat, a stronghold of the Mughals, as it was the closest accessible port on the west coast due to the landlocked territory. This marked Hawkins as the third Britisher to reach India. The first was Ralph Fitch, who visited the Mughal emperor Akbar in 1584 and later became a consultant to the company. The second was John Mildenhall, who arrived at the court of Akbar in 1603 and engaged in regular political discussions with him. He promised several expensive gifts to the emperor on his next visit. However, his visit was later declared unofficial as the company had not authorized him to travel to India.

William Hawkins (1811–14), from the Barden Collection, State Archives of North Carolina, Raleigh, N.C.[1]

Returning to the present in 1608, Hawkins discovered to his dismay that, effectively, the Surat port was under the control of the Portuguese. They were unlikely to permit rival ships to anchor there. The Portuguese wielded enormous influence over the Mughal emperor and consistently paid their tributes on time, in addition to presenting curious objects collected from their colonies all over the world. Despite introducing himself as an English ambassador, Hawkins lacked the requisite charisma and body language, leading to the discovery of his subterfuge. His arrival in Surat was met with anything but a warm welcome. Mukarrab Khan, the Mughal customs official overseeing the Gujarat ports, promptly seized the ship, its boats and a significant portion of the gifts. Furthermore, he ordered the arrest of many British sailors. Soon, Hawkins learned that the Portuguese had orchestrated these actions. He attempted to persuade the Portuguese, reminding them of the newfound friendship between England and Portugal after the cessation of war in 1604, urging them not to jeopardize it.

However, the Portuguese showed no inclination to extend an olive branch and instead resorted to vulgar insults. They disparaged England as 'an island of no import', King James as 'a king of fishermen' and dismissed Hawkins with contempt, referring to him as 'a fart for his commission'. Moreover, they asserted that the 'King of Portugal' owned all the ports between Persia and India, emphasizing that no one dared enter India without the Portuguese king's permission. Enraged by such language, Hawkins challenged them to a duel, but the Portuguese were uninterested in engaging in impractical theatrics. Instead, they promptly sent the British prisoners to Goa. Only Hawkins and his assistant, Finch, were permitted to remain free in Surat.[2]

Despite the Portuguese's attempts on his life, which he thwarted with his skill in swordplay, Hawkins and his companions were compelled to sell some of their precious merchandize to make ends meet. In the meantime, the captain managed to obtain a pass for their journey to Agra. Unfortunately, Finch fell sick, necessitating Hawkins to proceed alone towards Agra in February 1609. Along the way, he met the viceroy of the Deccan at Burhanpur, who received him warmly. They conversed in Turkish for three hours, and the viceroy accepted a gift from Hawkins. In return, he presented Hawkins with 'two Clokes, one of fine Woollen and another of Cloth of Gold; giving mee his most kind letter of favour to the King, which avayled much'.[3]

Due to the hazardous nature of travel, Hawkins enlisted the assistance of capable Pathans to provide protection and serve as guides. Being an employee of the EIC, his primary concern was obtaining the Mughal 'farman' (an irrevocable royal decree) issued by the king. Unfortunately, when Hawkins departed from England, he had been misinformed that Akbar was the reigning monarch. Upon reaching India, however, Hawkins discovered that Jahangir was the new emperor, about whom he possessed little knowledge.

Hawkins overlooked the lush green jungles during his journey to Agra and upon arrival, he remained unimpressed with the city, despite it being 'one of the biggest and richest cities in the world of the time'[4]. With his financial situation precarious, everything now depended on gaining favour with the Mughal emperor.

Finally arriving in Agra in April after ten arduous weeks filled with effort, toil and danger, Hawkins decided to keep a low profile initially, seeking some rest. However, word quickly spread that a white gentleman from distant lands had come to Agra. Jahangir took notice and promptly extended invitations for Hawkins to attend the court without delay. Hawkins's fortunes began to improve when Jahangir seemed visibly pleased upon meeting him. The Mughal emperors had a penchant for acquiring women of various races for their harems and men of diverse backgrounds for their courts, aiming to showcase their wealth and power. They harboured a fierce rivalry with the Ottoman sultans and sought to outdo them in every aspect.

The Mughal Empire stood at the pinnacle of its power and wealth during Jahangir's reign. Inheriting one of the world's two richest political systems – rivalled only by Ming China – from his father, Akbar, Jahangir's territory encompassed akhand (unbroken) Bharat, comprising Afghanistan, Pakistan, Nepal, Bhutan, Bangladesh and the majority of India. With a population of approximately 10 crore people, five times the number controlled by the Ottomans, the Mughals wielded unparalleled influence. Notably, they were the only Muslim rulers who did not remit one-fifth of their plunder to the Khalifa of Baghdad.

With a population of 15 crore people, roughly 20 per cent of the world's population, India, including Mughal and other kingdoms, produced 25 per cent of the world's manufactured goods at the time. In many respects, it was the world's industrial superpower and a pioneer in textile production. America can be seen as yesteryear's India. It's not without reason that numerous English words associated with weaving have Indian origins, including chintz, calico, shawl, pyjamas, khaki, dungarees, cummerbund and taffetas.[5]

The Mughal capitals of Agra and Delhi stood as the megacities of their time. According to Jesuit Fr Antonio Montserrate, who served in the durbar of Akbar, 'they are second to none either in Asia or in Europe regarding either size, population, or wealth'[6]. Merchants from across Asia converged in these cities, where every kind of art and craft was practised. The Mughal heartland witnessed an astounding influx of 18 metric tonnes of silver annually between 1586 and 1605, as noted by William Hawkins, 'All nations bring coyne and carry away commodities for the same.'[7]

Hawkins's gifts, though few in number, were well-received by the king, and he was accorded a respectful welcome with traditional Indian hospitality and kindness. Jahangir expressed increased happiness upon learning that more gifts would be forthcoming whenever ships from England anchored at Surat. However, Hawkins faced challenges as his letters were read in court with the assistance of a Portuguese Jesuit who attempted to prejudice the emperor against the British messenger. Hawkins experienced a moment of embarrassment when a letter from English King James I was incorrectly addressed to Emperor Akbar as the sultan of Surat. In defence of Hawkins, it was noted that the letter was five years old, and communication in those days was poor. Akbar had been deceased for three years, and Hawkins could sense the muffled laughter of the darbaris while the letter was being read. Fortunately, Jahangir did not take offence at the mistake, much to Hawkins's relief.

The Portuguese attempted to influence the emperor by downplaying the significance of Hawkins, portraying him as a mere visitor from a poor fishing nation of no consequence. However, Jahangir had different intentions, and Hawkins was escorted to a private room for further discussions. They conversed in Turkish, a language both Hawkins and Jahangir were fluent in, which helped cement their relationship. Hawkins was also provided with suitable accommodation befitting his status. The king enjoyed engaging in conversations with Hawkins about Europe over wine-filled evenings. Hawkins regaled the king with amusing European anecdotes, fostering a closer relationship. His importance gradually grew within the court, securing him a prominent position. Eventually, Jahangir preferred to have Hawkins be by his side, valuing their discussions on English and international affairs. Hawkins later wrote: 'Both night and day, his delight was very much to talk with mee, both of the Affaires of England and other Countries.'[8]

To maintain William Hawkins's favour, he was granted a salary equivalent to £3,200 per annum, appointed leader of 400 horses, bestowed the respectable rank of 'Khan' and granted permission for a factory at Surat. This marked the first formal recognition of English trade in India, a milestone that would be looked back upon only three centuries later, in 1947. Jahangir later affectionately nicknamed Hawkins the 'English Khan', much to the delight of the honest captain. Over time, Hawkins even started adopting Muslim attire and mannerisms.

Hawkins's Marriage

After a few months, Jahangir sensed a certain urgency in Hawkins. Believing that Hawkins might be in need of companionship, Jahangir offered him any white Caucasian girl from his harem. However, Hawkins perceived this as an attempt at conversion and expressed his preference for a Christian girl to the king. Jahangir, feeling it incumbent upon him as a Mughal king, vowed to find a suitable match from his harem. Indeed, a girl meeting Hawkins's exact specifications was discovered – an Armenian Christian girl. She epitomized the diversity of India, being a white Christian Armenian living among Turkish Muslims. Emperor Akbar had a fondness for Armenian Christians and had invited their traders to settle in Agra, where they were exempt from paying taxes. A church was even constructed in Agra in 1562, a novelty in northern India at that time.

In addition to arranging the marriage, Jahangir cautioned Hawkins of the potential danger to his life from the Portuguese, cautioning that he might be poisoned at any moment. He emphasized the importance of having a loyal wife to safeguard his food and life. Consequently, Hawkins and Mariam Khan were married according to Christian traditions, solidifying their bond and ensuring Hawkins's safety to the best of Jahangir's ability.

Christianity in Mughal Durbar

By the time of Akbar's reign, the Mughals had consolidated their rule in India, and they no longer harboured insecurities. The Mughals, who from the beginning were a line of warriors who 'ruled by the drawn sword', were now willing to temper their image by investing in the high cultural life of arts and architecture. They were even immune to blasphemy charges. Akbar's ambitions led to the annexation of Gujarat in 1573, bringing the Mughals into proximity with the Portuguese. The latter sought to maintain good relations with the Mughals as they needed both protection and permissions to set up more factories. Consequently, there was a growing presence of Europeans in the Mughal durbar. As gifts for the emperor, the Portuguese Jesuit missions from Goa presented numerous illustrated European books, paintings and inscriptions created by renowned artists. These illustrations were typically replete with biblical imagery. American historian Gauvin Bailey recounted this phenomenon:

> In open defiance of Islam's traditional abjuration of figural art, the Mughal royal family evinced an active interest in – and even open worship of – Catholic devotional images. Akbar ordered his artists to paint hundreds of iconic portraits of Jesus, Mary, and a panoply of Christian saints in the styles of the late Renaissance to adorn books, albums, jewelry, and even treaties.[9]

In Asia, particularly in India, the newly established Jesus Society emerged as a leading force in missionary work. They blended rigorous academic preparation with a missionary approach that emphasized tolerance and adaptation, contrasting with the fanaticism observed in other religious groups. However, it is worth noting that Christians themselves often resorted to violent methods in their efforts to convert Europe and the Americas. By framing their missionary endeavours as dialogues, the Jesuits gained a reputation for being adept debaters and were warmly received in the courts of the Mughals. This approach persisted into the British era and beyond, with Jesuits employing similar methods and achieving significant success in converting the entirety of Northeast India.

Soon, the durbar was adorned with numerous paintings and statues, prompting many Europeans to speculate that the Mughals were on the verge of conversion. However, the Mughals demonstrated their astuteness by incorporating elements of European artistic style into their own, thus pioneering a new genre known as Mughal art.

Akbar was known to have commissioned murals depicting Mary, Jesus and several Christian prophets for his royal palace at Fatehpur Sikri. Nevertheless, it was Jahangir who oversaw the commissioning of the largest number of devotional murals from

1608 until 1621. One probable explanation for the presence of Christian paintings in Mughal courts is that the Quran recognizes Jesus and Mary (Madonna) as two of their early prophets. Additionally, the Mughals may have been motivated to counter the visually rich Hindu imagery by incorporating Christian symbols, as Islam traditionally prohibits such visual representations. These commissioned paintings also served as a means to convey the divine approval of their rule to the populace. At a deeper level, this syncretic art represented the power and glory of the Mughal dynasty.

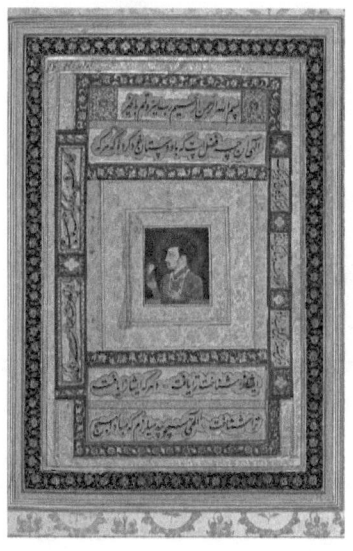

Jahangir holding the portrait of Madonna, c. 1620, now in National Museum, New Delhi.[10]

There was no doubt that among all the Mughals, Jahangir was the man most inclined towards Christianity. His life was dedicated to wine and women, and he had no interest whatsoever in conquering further lands in India. What is more, he did not have any interest in Islam either. In the evening, he used to have long sessions of merrymaking in which anything and everything was allowed. He even went so far as to eat pork, a dish especially prohibited in Islam. In the royal kitchen, it was not available, so he used to go to the homes of Jesuit fathers to eat it with wine. However, these activities did not go well with the mullahs, and they raised severe objections, which further offended the emperor. He asked them which religion allowed pork, to which they replied that only Christianity was such a religion.

Jahangir then publicly stated that he wanted to become a Christian, upon hearing which there was even more commotion. The maulanas then had an intense discussion and stated that the king might eat and drink whatever he liked. Probably he did not have any intention of converting but was having fun at their expense. Once, he ordered several figurines of pigs in solid gold and put them in front of his bed so that when he woke, he got to see them instead of any Muslim.

Jahangir even used to eat and drink during the daytime in the holy month of Ramadan in the royal durbar. He even went a step further and used to give some pieces of food to those who seemed to him to be the most fanatic. They had no other choice but to eat, as the emperor was fond of throwing such people to the hungry and angry lions of the royal zoo.

On other occasions, he made Jesuit fathers debate religious matters with mullahs, and it was always Christians who came out on top. Once during the debate, Joseph da Costa, a Portuguese father, responded with enthusiasm to a mullah: 'Here and now, I can prove to Your Majesty and the entire court that the gospel I hold in my hand is true. If Your Majesty orders a stack of straw to be brought here, I will sit on it with my book and the Qazi with his Quran. When we are seated, set the straw on fire and it will reveal which faith is true.' The Qazi, terrified by this proposal and aware of Jahangir's inclination to test such claims, turned pale, lowered his head and trembled so much that he soiled himself, filling the court with a foul odour. Jahangir and the courtiers held their noses in disgust. Jahangir then remarked, 'I see that the padre is willing to prove his faith, but the Qazi is already scared and has made a fool of himself.' He addressed the padre: 'From this day forth, you shall be known as "Padri Atash"—Father of Fire.'[11]

Certainly, Catholic influences began to decline following the arrival of Hawkins, a British Protestant, in 1608. Later, with the rise of fanatic Mughal kings like Shah Jahan and Aurangzeb, the era of syncretism experienced an abrupt demise.

Politics in the Mughal Durbar

As a year swiftly passed, Hawkins found himself the target of jealousy among the Muslim courtiers. How could a 'firangi', especially a Christian, gain such favour with the king in such a short time? Amidst this growing unrest, reports of additional English ships, though wrecked, docking at Surat began to circulate. Both darbaris and the Portuguese perceived this as a distinct threat and voiced their concerns. Hawkins's hopes sank along with his countenance as he had anticipated more gifts for the emperor, who, in turn, had high expectations of receiving rare collectibles. 'Let the English come no more,' said the emperor, weary of the ongoing strife.

Mukarrab Khan, the customs official, was summoned to court for giving fabricated evidence regarding the low value of gifts brought by Hawkins. However, Khan himself fell into disgrace when severe corruption charges were levied against him. Seeing an opportunity, Hawkins decided it was time to demand compensation for the goods looted by Khan upon the arrival of the ships at Surat, which still rankled him. He believed this was the reason he could not present appropriate gifts to the emperor. Khan argued that the quoted price for the goods was inflated, but Hawkins remained steadfast and threatened to bring the matter to the emperor's attention. Khan, lacking necessary funds, ultimately couldn't pay.

Khwaja Abul Hasan, the king's chief wazir, tried to mediate between the two parties, urging the Britisher to accept the offered compensation. Hawkins, however, refused to relent, and the complaint was lodged in the royal court. Jahangir, enraged by the incident, reluctantly ordered the remaining money to be paid from the royal treasury. This marked the first instance of Jahangir disapproving of Hawkins's behaviour, with Hasan also becoming his sworn enemy. Hawkins's insistence on the compensation was viewed as a misstep, as it resulted in strained relations with the court. Further incidents, mostly imaginary, were narrated in court, eroding the king's trust in Hawkins and leading him to consider the Englishman a liability.

The repercussions began swiftly. Hawkins found himself removed from the list of prominent courtiers. While he harboured resentment toward Wazir Hasan for this, deep down, he knew it had the emperor's approval. Furthermore, he was excluded from the drinking sessions with Jahangir, and his seating position at court was downgraded, a humiliation he could not bear. He became the subject of mockery, and his allowance was withheld. Overwhelmed by the deteriorating situation, he eventually petitioned the emperor – either reinstate him to his former status or grant him leave to depart.

The wrecked ship *Ascension*, that had docked in September 1609, a year after *Hector* anchored at Surat, brought with it several hundred sailors who remained in Surat. They frequented establishments with questionable reputations, indulging in low-quality wines and the company of women of ill repute. One day, an English sailor named Thomas Tucker committed a grave offence by killing a cow calf, an act considered more than a murder in India. This sparked outrage among the Hindus, who demanded retribution. Tucker was only spared when his fellow sailors intervened, rendering him unconsciousness. Subsequently, all the sailors, including Finch, were sent to Agra, but the harsh conditions of the journey proved fatal for many. These sailors bore witness to Hawkins's diminished standing at court. Meanwhile, almost all other Britishers, except Hawkins, returned to Surat in the hope of encountering a British ship that would facilitate their journey home.

During this time, Hawkins's reputation experienced a slight improvement when his arch-nemesis, Hasan the wazir, was reassigned to the Deccan. Hawkins received word that a new English fleet, led by Sir Henry Middleton, had docked at Surat on 26 September. This reignited his hopes for acquiring new gifts for the emperor. Hawkins presented Jahangir with a handsome ruby ring, which he had previously kept concealed, and the emperor's delight was palpable. Sensing an opportune moment, Hawkins once again requested a farman for setting up a factory. Jahangir, known for his emotional nature, immediately asked his clerk to draft it, but another courtier reminded the king of the promise not to grant rights to the English as they had done to the Portuguese when they brought expensive gifts to the Mughal court. Consequently, the emperor withdrew his initial approval. However, he assured Hawkins that he would seek a compromise and issue a charter soon. Upon learning of this incident, the Portuguese presented the emperor with more exotic goods, ensuring that Hawkins's former prominence remained elusive.

The politics of the Mughal court were draining Hawkins's energy, as it seemed that everyone was conspiring against him. Various factions within the durbar were attempting to poison the king's mind – the Portuguese due to his English origin, the Jesuits because he did not belong to their sect and the Muslim darbaris, who were enraged by the preferential treatment afforded to a Christian.

In such a dire situation, Hawkins committed yet another blunder, one that would leave no room for forgiveness. Later, he would count himself lucky for escaping with his life. In the middle of 1611, Hawkins instructed Finch to buy indigo from Bayana, located approximately 100 km away from Agra. In between, the emperor's mother also sought to purchase indigo for resale and to offer as gifts to other kings on her journey to Mecca. She owned a fleet of large ships that traversed the pilgrim route to Mecca, with the port of Jedda serving as a bustling hub for global trade. Among her fleet, the *Rahimi* was the largest vessel engaged in commerce. Unaware of her identity, Finch outbid her for the indigo stock. Infuriated, the mother demanded that Jahangir immediately expel Hawkins from India, a decree that was promptly executed. Simultaneously, the authorization to establish the factory at Surat was revoked under pressure from the Portuguese viceroy; however, permission for a trading post remained intact.

Hawkins packed his bags and left Agra with his wife and her jewels in November 1611, following more than two years of residence there without substantial achievements. After three months, he reached Surat. Initially, his in-laws opposed his departure, so he evaded them by falsely claiming he was headed to Goa. He sailed home several months later, in February 1612, aboard a ship bound for Bantam, Indonesia, but died en route near London in April 1613.

His wife did not remain without companionship for long. She swiftly became involved in a passionate relationship with Gabriel Towerson, a handsome sailor on the ship. Mariam later married him, and after two years of living in London, they returned to India in 1617. In the process, she became the first Indian woman to officially immigrate to England. On their return voyage to India, another agent of the company named Richard Steele accompanied by his wife Frances was aboard the ship. Since the company policy still prohibited women from boarding, she disguised herself as Mariam's maid. Complicating matters further was her advanced pregnancy. When Thomas Roe, the next official to India, found out, he was upset but unable to take action due to the delicate circumstances. However, more setbacks befell Mariam. Towerson, while returning to England in 1619, abandoned her. Subsequently, Mariam made several appeals to the company for support, but to no avail. Towerson died a few years later, in 1623, during the Dutch massacre of the British known as the Massacre of Amboyna, and his property was awarded to his brothers.

Hawkins as Reviewed by His Peers

William Finch, his only full-time colleague in India, often quarrelled with him about his wayward decision-making. Finch termed him enterprising and resourceful but also somewhat arrogant and outspoken. Hawkins failed to leave a favourable impression on his peers. Another contemporary, John Jourdain, gave a critical portrayal of his behaviour, stating that 'his promises were of little force, for he was very fickle in his resolution, as also in his religion'. Although Thomas Roe did not know him personally, he wrote of him, 'For Hawkings, I fynd him a vayne foole.'[12]

Hawkins so greatly angered Jahangir that the emperor did not mention him in his autobiography, *Jahangirnama*. However, he did not reference Roe either. In the Mughal scheme of things, the British held a negligible position.

Overall, Hawkins failed to learn the nuances of diplomacy concerning Mughal rulers, including the protocols and etiquettes required in court.

His Memoirs

Though Hawkins was not a traveller in the strictest sense, as he visited to promote his company's business interests, his memoirs were published alongside other travellers' accounts in the book *Early Travels in India, 1583–1619*, edited by William Foster. He described his journey to India, with a primary focus on the politics of the Mughal palace.

He documented Jahangir's daily rituals, having found himself in an enviable position due to his close proximity to the emperor and residence within the palace. He was astounded by Jahangir's habit of drinking six glasses of alcohol, as prescribed by his doctor, along with some opium in the evening. Eventually, the emperor would become so intoxicated that his attendants had to open his mouth and force-feed him. Hawkins also quoted a statement of Jahangir regarding the British, 'An Englishman withouten a stronge drinke is like a fysshe out of water.'

The daily routine of Emperor Jahangir scarcely enriched the lives of his subjects. He would rise, present himself to onlookers and then retired to the harem again. Following a few hours of court proceedings, it was time for him to witness elephant fights and other sporting events. In the evening, he would attend to various grievances and complaints for an hour or so. As the sun set on the horizon, wine flowed copiously. Hawkins noted:

> He eateth a bit to stay his stomach, drinking once of his stronge drinke. Then he cometh forth into a private roome, where none can come but such as himself nominateth (for two yeeres I was one of his attendants here).[13]

In his account, Hawkins also wrote of his wife, '[She was] of the race of most ancient Christians', and for that reason alone, he married her.[14]

The forbidden chambers of the harem always fascinated European travellers, and Hawkins was no exception. During his two-year stay in the palace, he must have seen and heard rumours about the harem. There were approximately 5,000 women in Jahangir's harem, separated from the 300 royal wives by sturdy doors.

Additionally, there were 1,000 young men and eunuch in the harem, should the emperor desire a robust physique someday. Hawkins also referred to the extraordinary expenses of maintaining the harem. According to him, 'The expenses daily for his [King's] women by the day is thirty thousand rupia.'[15]

Though Hawkins saw the Mughals closely, his memoirs lacked incisiveness, probably indicating he was not a keen observer. Nevertheless, there is a wealth of first-hand evidence that no historian of India can afford to ignore. He noted that courtiers were ranked based on the number of horses they owned and received salaries from the royal treasury accordingly. Upon their deaths, all their property went to the emperor, and 'all the lands belong to him', but 'commonly he dealeth well' with their children. The king's yearly income was estimated at Rs 50 crore.[16]

Hawkins portrayed Jahangir as the greatest emperor of the East due to his wealth, vast land holdings and formidable military strength. He described the royal treasury, which housed countless gold plates and jewels, including 500 drinking cups, some crafted from 'one piece of Ballace Ruby'. Hawkins estimated that at least 36,000 servants, gardeners, grooms and others attended the court. The royal stable boasted of 12,000 elephants, with 300 reserved for the emperor's personal use. Daily court expenses amounted to Rs 50,000. Besides elephants, the royal 'zoo' also had 10,000 oxen, 2,000 camels, 3,000 deer, 4,000 dogs, 100 tame lions, 500 buffaloes and 10,000 carrier pigeons.[17]

Hawkins describes Jahangir as unpopular among his subjects, who 'stand in great fear of him', ascribing it to his innate cruelty. He showed a preference for Muslims over Hindus for top positions in the court, resulting in very few Hindus occupying prominent roles. Jahangir took pleasure in gruesome spectacles, such as men being torn apart by elephants, with elephant fights being his favourite entertainment five days a week. On mere suspicion, he was reputed to have killed his secretary with his bare hands and lashed a man almost to death for merely breaking a dish. He took delights in spectacles involving fights between men and animals, once forcing an unarmed man to fight a lion until he was ripped to shreds. This cruelty, combined with a corrupt and unkind government, resulted in discontent among his subjects. Highways became infested with criminals, and numerous rebellions erupted.[18]

Hawkins's narrative combines elements of autobiography, travelogue and geographical investigation, evoking a range of emotions from respect and poise to contempt and misunderstanding.

Epilogue

After Hawkins's departure, both bravery and luck favoured the English. The Portuguese, who by then had a complete monopoly over the shipping lanes of the Arabian Sea on the western coast of India, faced a new challenge. Under the command of Thomas Best, the ship *Red Dragon* embarked on the East India Company's tenth voyage. In September 1612, Best secured trading rights for the company at Surat and, two months later, engaged a Portuguese fleet, defeating and driving them from the Gulf of Cambay at the Battle of Swally.

Impressed by the English and recognizing their potential to counter the Portuguese monopoly, Emperor Jahangir, who lacked a navy, granted the English permission in early 1613 to establish a factory at Surat. By January of the next year, Best had successfully set up a factory there and extended trade to Ahmedabad, Burhanpur and Agra.

Due to the increased arrogance of the Portuguese stemming from their monopoly on Indian waters, every Asian ship had to obtain a *cartaz*, or pass, by paying customs at a Portuguese port or by maintaining an agent in residence there. The pass listed all the ports the ship was allowed to visit and the specific articles of trade it could carry. If a ship did not have the pass or violated its conditions, it could be seized by any Portuguese patrol. Particularly objectionable to traditional Muslims was that each pass bore images of the Virgin Mary and Jesus. For Muslims, especially those on pilgrimage, travelling under such conditions would mean condoning idolatry. Many orthodox Muslims sometimes suspended their obligation to pilgrimage. However, during the relatively tolerant periods of Akbar and Jahangir, pilgrimage to Mecca continued robustly despite these religious challenges.

Over time, the Portuguese acquired a reputation for considerable brutality. Their actions included robbery at sea, diverting Arab and other trade away from the subcontinent, imposing curbs on the export of goods and thus stunting the local industry. Their persistent evangelizing at every level and stinginess in giving gifts to the Mughal court further eroded Indian goodwill. These factors eventually led the Mughals to seek out other trading partners.

Nevertheless, the Portuguese managed to keep Jahangir in good humour by showering him with rare, expensive curios from around the world, and he either ignored their indiscretions or accommodated them. However, this changed in 1613. A large and well-known pilgrimage ship named the *Rahimi*, owned by Jahangir's mother, Jodha Bai, was seized by the Portuguese at Surat. The ship, carrying Hajj pilgrims and their goods worth £1 lakh in today's currency, along with seven hundred people on board, was taken to Goa. Despite carrying the necessary pass and not violating any of its terms, the Portuguese, driven by greed or anger at the new Mughal alliance with the English, acted purely out of revenge. The ship was later burned down, along with

119 other vessels. This event marked a great upheaval and signalled a shift in the balance of power: 'This is a Hindu empress' Muslim ship, carrying Hajj pilgrims in Christian waters patrolled by the Portuguese armada.'[19]

Upon hearing of this catastrophe, Jahangir flew into a rage, closed all the churches in his territory, and suspended the scholarships of Portuguese priests. He then sent his army to raid their important colony of Daman.

Faced with the might of the Mughal army, the Portuguese had no choice but to offer a truce. They paid Rs 3 lakh for the ship along with other gifts. However, they also demanded the expulsion of the British, a demand which Jahangir refused.

From this point on, Portuguese influence declined while the British became favoured. King James I wasted no time and dispatched Thomas Roe to India as England's first official envoy from 1615 to 1618.

By now, Europeans knew the Mughals' fascination for exotic and rare objects, wines and opium, having gained considerable insight from previous visits. Roe was tasked with completing what Hawkins had only partially accomplished. However, English traders still found themselves in a deplorable situation, enduring various forms of abuses without any legal protection. Englishmen were openly scorned, robbed, arrested and even physically assaulted in the streets by individuals like peons and porters. Their leaders, EIC agents, had brought disgrace upon their nation by 'kotowing' to Moghul dignitaries, enduring insults without asserting any semblance of dignity.[20]

Though Hawkins may have been considered a failure, a fact he likely recognized himself, he could never have imagined in his wildest dreams that his efforts would ultimately lead to the British Empire's dominion over India, a mere century and a half later.

'The East Offering Its Riches to Britannia', an oil painting by Spyridon Romas.[21]

William Hawkins's journey to the court of the Mughal Emperor Jahangir was fraught with challenges and ultimately ended in failure. However, the British East India Company did not abandon their ambitions in India. Instead, they learned from his experience and modified their strategies, eventually establishing a powerful and lasting presence in India.

Hawkins's mission highlighted the importance of understanding and respecting Mughal customs and court etiquette. Future British envoys, like Sir Thomas Roe, were better prepared and more culturally sensitive. Roe took great care to learn Persian, understand Mughal court politics and present himself in a respectful manner that appealed to the emperor. Mistakes, such as the issue of a royal letter to Akbar three years after his death, were never repeated.

Moreover, Hawkins's failure also demonstrated the importance of presenting valuable gifts and establishing trade relations to gain favour. The British realized that to engage successfully with the Mughals, they needed to offer items of interest, such as fine English goods, and promise profitable trade opportunities. This approach helped create a more positive impression and facilitated negotiations.

Additionally, Hawkins's unsuccessful mission emphasized the necessity of military strength in protecting British interests. The East India Company began building a private army to safeguard their factories and assert their dominance. This military presence allowed them to protect their trade routes and interests from rival European powers and local threats. Thomas Best's naval victory over the Portuguese at the Battle of Swally demonstrated their rapid learning curve.

Simultaneously, fortune also favoured the British. The burning of the *Rahimi* marked a turning point, after which the British never looked back. The Mughal rout of the Portuguese in the aftermath ensured that instead of seeking immediate and large-scale control, the British opted for incremental expansion.

Sir Thomas Roe standing before the Great Moghul, c. 1615.[22]

Denouement: A Company that Ruled over the World

The efforts of Hawkins, though unsuccessful, eventually led to the EIC, rather than the British government, conquering India in the mid-18th century. This unregulated private enterprise, headquartered in a small London office with only five windows, was administered in India by ruthless governors-general and viceroys. Despite its small administrative team – just thirty-five full-time employees at its headquarters – the EIC epitomized corporate efficiency in many ways. In its century-long existence, the company amassed its own armed forces comprising a staggering 260,000 soldiers, twice the size of the British army at the time. With its formidable military might, it wielded more firepower than any nation-state in Asia, essentially functioning as 'an empire within an empire'. Although it took nearly 150 years to assert control over Bengal, the EIC's dominance endured until 1947, when India gained independence.

The Mughal emperor Shah Alam hands over the Treaty of Allahabad to Robert Clive.[23]

The first major victory was the Battle of Plassey in 1757, where the EIC defeated the nawab of Bengal. This victory was swiftly followed by another at the Battle of Buxar in 1764, resulting in the Treaty of Allahabad in 1765. Under this treaty, Mughal king Shah Alam granted the company 'Diwani rights', authorizing it to collect taxes on behalf of the emperor from the people of Bengal, Bihar and Orissa. With increased economic power, the company implemented financial regulations that allowed them to exploit the region's resources for personal gain. This marked a pivotal moment in Indian history, so humiliating that a Mughal official named Narayan Singh remarked afterwards, 'When we have to take orders from a handful of traders who have not yet learned to wash their bottoms?'[24]

It was reported that Clive had personally drafted the Treaty of Allahabad, and a frightened Shah Alam just signed it. The Mughal historian Sayyid Ghulam Husain Khan observed:

> A business of such magnitude, as left neither pretence nor subterfuge, and which at any other time would have required the sending of wise ambassadors and able negotiators, as well as much parley and conference with the East India Company and the King of England, and much negotiation and contention with the ministers, was done and finished in less time than would usually have been taken up for the sale of a jack-ass, or a beast of burden, or a head of cattle. [25]

Clive later transferred no less than £2.5 million from the defeated rulers of Bengal to the EIC treasury, which, in today's terms, equates to about £23 million for Clive personally and £250 million for the company. English author Horace Walpole scoffed at this plunder in 1790, 'What is England now? A sink of Indian wealth ... filled by nabobs [with] ... a Senate sold and despised.'[26]

The first baron, Edward Thurlow (1731–1806), the lord chancellor, during the impeachment of Warren Hastings, castigated the corporations, saying, 'Corporations have neither bodies to be punished, nor souls to be condemned, they therefore do as they like.'[27]

It's understandable why the company billed itself as 'the grandest society of merchants in the Universe'. Its power had spread around the world, and by the end of the 18th century, its armies surpassed those of nearly every nation-state. In fact, its shares had become a form of global reserve currency by this point. British MP, philosopher and historian, Edward Burke stated that the company's constitution 'began in commerce and ended in empire', or, as one of its directors put it, 'an empire within an empire'.[28]

Throughout its history, the EIC never had more than 5,000 white officers and 50,000 white soldiers to govern over 10 crore Indians. The majority of these soldiers were Indian. Military conquest, plunder and exploitation of India continued unchecked until 1858, when the British government assumed governance of India. However, this does imply that the British government proved to be any better. Over the course of their rule, it's conservatively estimated that they looted $45 trillion (in today's value) from India. According to economic historian Robert C. Allen, extreme poverty in India amplified from 23 per cent in 1810 to over 50 per cent in the mid-20th century under British rule. During the 200 years of British rule, an estimated 10 crore Indians perished due to famines, wars and torture. The scale of plunder was so immense that the Sanskrit word 'loot' became the first word to be entered in the English dictionary. The British can be viewed as the original corporate raiders. One estimate suggests that India's per capita income was four times that of the Britain's around 1600. However, by the time they left India in 1947, Britain's per capita income was four times greater than that of Indians, illustrating the extent of the drain of wealth from India. Historian Mike Davis contended that Britain's imperial policies 'were often the exact moral equivalents of bombs dropped from 18,000 feet'.[29]

It is perhaps the largest act of corporate violence in history.

6

Jean-Baptiste Tavernier

'In all my travels, I have never seen a people so fond of precious stones as the Indians.'

—Jean-Baptiste Tavernier

Jean-Baptiste Tavernier (1605–89) was a prominent French diamond merchant and traveller of the 17th century, best known for his extensive travels across Asia and the invaluable insights he provided into the cultures and commerce of the region. Born in Paris, Tavernier hailed from a family of successful merchants and embarked on a series of voyages that significantly influenced European understanding of the East.

Tavernier embarked on his most notable journeys between 1631 and 1668, during which he covered extensive ground, exploring various regions of Asia such as India, Persia and the Ottoman Empire. Over the course of these adventures, spanning approximately forty years, Tavernier covered a massive distance of 180,000 miles. Due to his extensive travels, he earned the epithet, Sindbad of the 17th century. His travels were motivated by a combination of commercial interests and a genuine curiosity about the diverse cultures and markets of the East.

Among Tavernier's voyages, his second journey stands out. Spanning from September 1638 to 1643, he travelled via Aleppo to Persia, then continued to India, reaching as far as Agra, and eventually journeyed to the kingdom of Golconda. At the court of Emperor Shah Jahan, Tavernier made his first visit to the diamond mines of Golconda. One of Tavernier's most significant contributions was his keen observations and documentation of the gem trade in India. He acquired an impressive collection of gems; Tavernier is renowned for purchasing the 116-carat Blue Diamond in 1666, which that later became known as the 'Hope Diamond'. Following Tavernier's initiation of diamond export to Europe, they became popular for use in engagement rings, symbolizing the rarity, beauty and durability that reflected the longevity of marriage.[1]

His writings, particularly the multivolume work titled *Les Six Voyages de Jean-Baptiste Tavernier* (*The Six Voyages of Jean-Baptiste Tavernier*), proved invaluable to European merchants, jewellers and scholars interested in the East. It became a bestseller and was translated into German, Dutch, Italian and English during his lifetime.

Tavernier's role extended beyond that of a mere merchant; he also operated as a de facto ambassador and diplomat. His extensive travels brought him into contact with various rulers and dignitaries, including Louis XIV of France and Shah Jahan of the Mughal Empire. His adeptness at navigating different cultural contexts and forging relationships with influential figures significantly contributed to his success as both a traveller and a trader.

Despite facing numerous challenges, such as shipwrecks, robberies and political turmoil, Tavernier's ventures proved to be highly profitable commercially. His writings provided Europeans detailed accounts of the economic and cultural landscapes of the East, fostering a better understanding of these regions. Tavernier's legacy extends beyond his contributions to commerce and gemmology; he is remembered as a chronicler who facilitated dialogue between the East and the West during a pivotal period in history.

Early Life and Wanderlust

Jean-Baptiste Tavernier in an oriental costume, 1679.[2]

Tavernier's father, a cartographer, crafted and sold maps. He had migrated from Paris to Antwerp, Belgium, following the massacre of thousands of Protestants by Catholics in France. Between 1562 and 1598, approximately thirty lakh people died due to violence, famines or diseases stemming from conflicts between the two Christian sects. Contrary to prevailing narratives, Christians often displayed levels of cruelty comparable to, if not surpassing, those attributed to Muslims.

Catholics killing Protestants in France in the 17th century.[3]

Later, his parents chose to return to Paris when the Edict of Nantes was issued, providing protection to Protestants. Tavernier's father's shop attracted many merchants, researchers and travellers, who shared stories of the world's unfolding events in Europe over the past two centuries. These stories were often narrated during family dinners, fuelling Tavernier's imagination with dreams. As soon as he entered his teenage years, he felt the stirrings of wanderlust. By the age of twenty-two, he claimed to have 'seen the best parts of Europe, France England, Holland, Germany ... and I spoke fairly the languages which are the most necessary'.[4]

Tavernier was familiar with the accounts of Marco Polo, a renowned 13th-century Venetian traveller, which were widely available throughout Europe. In his travelogue, Polo wrote:

Diamonds are only found in the Indian kingdom of Motupalli, where there are mountains with certain great and deep valleys, to the bottom of which there is no access. Wherefore, the men who go in search of diamonds take with them pieces of flesh, as lean as they can get, and these they cast into the bottom of a valley. Now there are numbers of white eagles that haunt those mountains and feed upon the serpents. When the eagles see the meat thrown down they pounce upon it and carry it up to some rocky hilltop where they begin to rend it. But there are men on the watch, and as soon as they see that the eagles have settled they raise a loud shouting to drive them away. And when the eagles are thus frightened away, the men recover the pieces of meat, and find them full of diamonds which have stuck to the meat down in the bottom. For the abundance of diamonds down there in the depths of the valleys is astonishing, but nobody can get down; and if one could, it would only be to be incontinently devoured by the serpents which are so rife there.

There is also another way of getting the diamonds. The people go to the nests of those white eagles, of which there are many, and in their droppings they find plenty of diamonds which the birds have swallowed in devouring the meat that was cast into the valleys. And, when the eagles themselves are taken, diamonds are found in their stomachs.

Indian diamonds 'are found both abundantly and of large size. Those that are brought to our part of the world are only the refuse, as it were, of the finer and larger stones.' [5]

The earliest diamonds were discovered in India in the 4th century BCE. At that time, diamonds were exclusively found in India, as the mines in Brazil and South Africa had yet to be discovered. Given the immense profitability of the Indian diamond trade in India, there was widespread demand for these precious gems. Early in human history, diamonds were used as engraving tools and later to adorn various deities in temples. Additionally, they served as talismans to ward off various evils. In Hindu culture, diamonds were believed to absorber negative energy, leading Hindu kings to favour wearing large diamonds. Upon extraction from the mines, these diamonds were often left uncut to preserve their perceived their purity. Most of these early stones were transported along the Silk Road. However, during the four centuries of Turkish rule, Indians found themselves without control over their lives, let alone diamonds. Diamonds became a risk-free loot for all.

After hearing all these stories, Tavernier grew increasingly fascinated with the thought of visiting India, which beckoned him to its pristine shores thousands of miles away. As mentioned earlier, between 1631 and 1668, he undertook six voyages to the region with the intention of procuring and trading Indian diamonds. He did so without any government backing or financial support. Relying solely on his resourcefulness, Tavernier organized transportation and lodging, exchanged currencies, secured credit and safeguarded both himself and his precious diamonds. He also acquired the knowledge necessary to navigate taxes, customs and tolls as he traversed the borders of various regional kingdoms.

While Tavernier did relish luxury at times, he also had to endure demanding journeys on modest-sized ships and gruelling treks by caravans. He even managed to survive a shipwreck and a period of imprisonment. Within India itself, he covered approximately 20,000 miles over the years, primarily utilizing small oxen-drawn carriages, bullock carts, horses or travelling by foot.

To escape the scorching heat, Tavernier often journeyed at night and rested at traveller's lodges overseen by local authorities. While some of these lodges were elaborate, most offered only basic amenities like food and shelter. Tavernier encountered both the protection and companionship of fellow travellers and occasional hostility upon reaching new destinations. However, his remarkable success in the diamond trade earned him respect and admirations from numerous prominent and minor rulers across Europe, the Persian Gulf, the Arabian Peninsula, India and Southeast Asia.

First Voyage

In 1631, Tavernier accompanied the entourage of French travellers, comprising two French fathers, M. de Chapes and M. de St Liebau, on a journey to Constantinople, Turkey. After an eleven-month stay there, he continued on to Isfahan, Persia. Tavernier then made his way back to Paris in 1633, travelling through Baghdad, Aleppo, Alexandretta, Malta and Italy.

Second Voyage

During his second voyage, which spanned from September 1638 to 1643, Tavernier travelled to Persia via Aleppo, Syria. He then proceeded to Agra to meet Emperor Shah Jahan. From Agra, he journeyed to visit the diamond mines in Golconda.

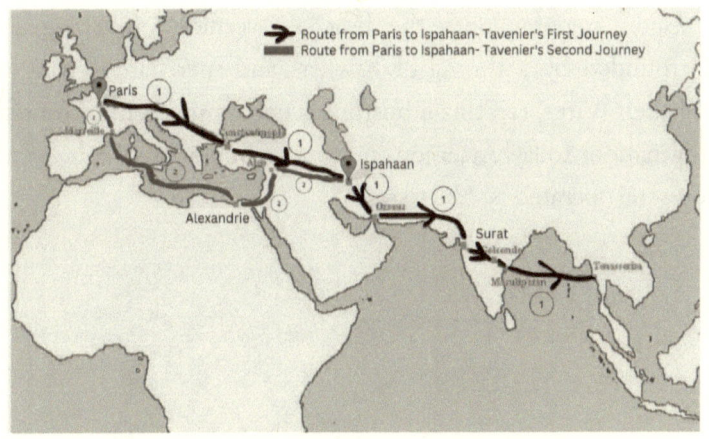

Routes of Tavernier's first and second voyages.[6]

On 13 September 1638, he boarded an east-bound ship from Paris accompanied by a doctor and his brother Daniel. With improved financial circumstances, he set out well-equipped as a merchant. After enduring a journey of one and a half years, his ship dropped anchor at Suvali, also known as Swally Hole by the British, a newly established port near Surat, in April 1640. Manucci would take the same route a decade later. The British fortified the port following a minor skirmish with the Portuguese in 1612, which holds historical significance as it marked the beginning of the rise of the EIC in India. In this historic clash, Thomas Best, captain of the British ship *Red Dragon*, outmanoeuvred and defeated the formidable Portuguese fleet, earning him the admiration and praise of the Mughal Emperor Jahangir. The battle persuaded the EIC to deploy a naval force to protect their commercial interests against various adversaries, including the Mughals, other European powers and pirates. Despite remaining accessible to the Mughals along the west coast, the port of Surat, unlike ports further south, fell under Portuguese control. This modest start is regarded as the foundation of the modern Indian Navy. Regrettably, the port no longer exists today.

Upon stepping onto the beach, Tavernier found himself surrounded by a throng of hawkers and merchants vying to sell their wares, creating a bustling scene reminiscent of tourist destinations today. After jostling with them for a while, he went to a serai operated by EIC to rest.

An illustrated map of the Persian Gulf with trees, plants and ships. These maps were instrumental in exploring and colonizing the world.[7]

Afterwards, he went to acquire local currency for meeting his expenses. In those days, all the imported gold and silver destined for India underwent melting and reminting into golden rupees, the only currency of Mughal India. This process adhered to a standard procedure overseen by the daroga at the customs office. Nothing transpired without greasing his palms, a practice that persists to this day. In this regard, India remains unchanged even after four centuries.[8]

En route to Surat, Tavernier found a huge English factory bustling with Hindu servants. He stayed there for a night but was abruptly awakened by a loud din. The same commotion he found at the beach was now happening at the factory gates, as people clamoured to proclaim their cotton rates at the top of their lungs. Tavernier observed that the majority of Hindus were shabbily dressed, with only a dhoti, essentially a loincloth, to cover themselves.

In the evening, Tavernier met William Fremlin, the English president of the EIC, and they quickly became friends when the president learned that Tavernier had come to deal in diamonds. During those days, all EIC employees were paid a meagre income, and to supplement their earnings, they were allowed to engage in side business. The only condition was not to carry goods back to England. To circumvent this, they dealt in diamonds, which could be easily concealed. In this situation, Tavernier positioned himself as an easy conduit to transport the diamonds.

After spending a night, Tavernier travelled from Surat to Agra via Ahmadabad in 1640. At Agra, he encountered Shah Jahan, reigning over Hindustan and levying exorbitant taxes to support his lavish lifestyle. From Agra, Tavernier embarked on a long and gruelling journey to Golconda, situated in what is now Andhra Pradesh and Telangana. Despite diamond markets being present in Goa or Agra, Tavernier reasoned that it would be more advantageous to procure diamonds at the source, where one could obtain better quality gems at a favourable price.

As the roads were infested with thugs and robbers, Tavernier enlisted thirty armed guards and ten servants to accompany him.

He eventually arrived at Rammalakota, a village near Kurnool in Andhra Pradesh, renowned as the hub of diamond mines. Situated in the Kolloru belt between the Krishna and Tungabhadra rivers, this area yielded many exceptional historic diamonds, including the rare Type IIa diamonds such as Kohinoor, Darya-i-Nur, Dresden Green, Empress Eugenie, Florentine, the pink Hortensia, Nassak, Nizam, Orlov, Pigot, Regent or Pitt, Sancy, Star of the East and the Great Mughal diamond (renowned for possessing the most pristine carbon crystal structure and chemical composition found in nature). Consequently, the Krishna River earned the moniker the Diamond River, or Adamas River, as the Greeks had named it. Upon Tavernier's arrival, he found at least 60,000 workers mining the diamonds.[9]

After much negotiation, Tavernier managed to purchase a substantial quantity of diamonds at reasonable prices. He was cautious not to offer excessively high prices, which could disrupt the market, nor too low to deter the dealers. However, in hindsight, they only cost him a fraction, considering the significant profits he later made by selling them at multiples.

One more surprising thing was that most of the native diamond dealers knew the Portuguese language; perhaps Portuguese nationals were among the first to reach there to mine the diamonds. One day, a man named Hiresh Dhawan, dressed in torn clothes, came to sell diamonds, whom Tavernier's assistant wanted to shoo away. However, Tavernier knew that outward appearances were often deceptive. The man offered him some rare gems but quoted a price much lower than reasonable. When the Frenchman asked him the reason, he started crying and explained that his son was on his deathbed, and doctors were unable to cure him. He then requested Tavernier to send a doctor, which he promptly did. After a correct diagnosis, the son indeed started to recover, and both men became lifelong friends. The man wanted to present Tavernier with a 48-carat diamond worth Rs 50,000, but Tavernier declined and paid a reasonable price. It was a friendship that would prove invaluable to him many times over the value of that single diamond.

In 1642, during a second trip to Golconda, Tavernier was offered a long, flat gem known as the Great Table, weighing 242 5/16 carats and possessing a delicate rose tint. It far surpassed the weight of the largest diamond in Europe, the Florentine, a 138-carat yellow diamond owned by the Grand Duke of Tuscany, with its hue inclining toward yellow. The asking price was Rs 500,000 (equivalent to 750,000 livres; French currency was weaker in those days). Tavernier sent a drawing to Fremlin, the EIC president, who suggested a reasonable price of Rs 400,000, but the owner declined it. Although Tavernier desired it desperately, he did not have the requisite capital and left greatly disappointed.

In November 1642, he went back to Paris via Surat.

Third Voyage

On his third journey (1643–49), he once more arrived in Surat via Aleppo and Isfahan in January 1645. From there, he revisited the Golconda diamond mines via Daulatabad. Over the next two years, Tavernier continued to visit different places in India, although little is known about his activities during this period.

In 1647, he departed for Isfahan but returned to India after a few months and landed at the port of Vengurla, north of Goa, on 20 January 1648. He wrote in his memoirs that the Inquisition was in full swing at that time, and every heathen was brutally tortured and killed. Most of the barbarity was reserved for Hindus, or, as they were called, the people of the beastly religion. About 15 lakh Hindus were murdered in Goa from 1516 until 1812 in a massacre during the Goa Inquisition. After arrests, thousands of people were never seen again. The atrocities committed by the Turks pale in comparison to those carried out by the Portuguese. They came to India with a cross in one hand and a sword in the other.

As usual, Hindus were the most affected in their own country, followed by Muslims. However, even Christians, primarily Protestants from various sects, were routinely tortured and jailed. In comparison to Hindus, the treatment of Muslims and Christians was relatively gentler.

The architect of the Inquisition was Francis Xavier, who singled out Brahmins for the killings and often quoted cruel verses from the Bible, which seem to be no different from those in the Quran: 'From an unholy race, wicked and crafty men, deliver me Lord.'[10]

Tavernier was also interrogated about his religion, despite it being common knowledge that he was a French Christian. During his two-month stay in Goa, he befriended the viceroy, Dom Philippe de Mascarenhas, and observed that in every town controlled by the Portuguese settlers, an officer was always in charge of making reports or arresting suspects and transporting them to Goa, where the head of the Inquisition was stationed. This was just the beginning of the process, hinting at what was to come:

> When the Inquisition seizes any person he is at once searched, and all that is found in his house in the way of furniture and effects, belonging to him, is inventoried to be returned to him should he be found innocent. But as regards anything of the nature of gold, silver, or jewels, it is not written down, and is never seen again, being taken to the Inquisitor for the expenses of the trial.[11]

Tavernier recounted a funny anecdote involving the Portuguese:

> The Portuguese who go to India have no sooner passed the Cape of Good Hope than they all become Fidalgos or gentlemen, and add Dom to the simple name of Pedro or Jeronimo which they carried when they embarked; this is the reason why they are commonly called in derision 'Fidalgos of the Cape of Good Hope.' As they change in their status so also they change in their nature....[13]

Christians demolishing a temple during the Goa Inquisition in the 17th century.[12]

Later, he journeyed to Ceylon and then to Indonesia before returning to France. During the voyage back, his ship had to make a three-week stop at the Cape in December 1648, as most of the sailors were infected with scurvy, a disease caused by a deficiency of vitamin C. Scurvy was the most dreaded disease of the time, particularly affecting sailors who subsisted on a diet devoid of fruits or vegetables, consisting solely of meat. Between 1500 and 1800, during the Age of Exploration, scurvy claimed the lives of at least twenty lakh sailors, by conservative estimates. Only 50 per cent of sailors typically survived the gruelling months-long voyages.

Fourth Voyage

On 2 July 1652, Tavernier reached the Indian city of Masulipatam, a port on the Bay of Bengal, now situated in the Krishna basin, approximately 200 miles from the diamond mines at Golconda, Andhra Pradesh. His purpose was to sell some of his expensive gems. The sultan of Golconda had a prime minister named Mir Jumla, who inspected all goods before purchasing them. Jumla was known more for his commercial acumen than his political role as a prime minister.

Aurangzeb's favourite general, Mir Jumla, shown in his harem.[14]

The story of Mir Jumla is nothing short of folklore. Born into privilege in Persia, he was the son of a prosperous oil merchant. From his youth, he was captivated by stories of the diamond mines of Golconda, where the famous Kohinoor diamond had once been excavated. Through his father's influential connections with Golconda's rulers, he secured a modest position as a clerk in the mines. Over time, he not only demonstrated remarkable skills but also acquired several mines, amassing considerable wealth. To facilitate his burgeoning business ventures, he delved into ship ownership, enabling trade with distant lands such as Arabia and Indonesia via sea routes. His talents soon captured the attention of Golconda's rulers, ultimately leading to his appointment as the vizier, or prime minister, of the region.

The Kollur mines, located along the Krishna River and now under Mir Jumla's jurisdiction, were the largest in Golconda, elevating him to become the wealthiest individual in the region. He leased these mines to his relatives and friends, while reserving the most significant and flawless gemstones for himself. These mines employed a workforce of 60,000 people, including men, women and children, and produced gemstones ranging from 40 to 900 carats in weight. The mining operation followed a structure similar to that of the Raolkooda mines in Bijapur, Karnataka, where contractors paid a 2 per cent ad valorem royalty to the government and obtained permission for excavation. It remains uncertain whether Mir Jumla's mines yielded other gems like agate, topaz, amethyst, etc., but he was renowned as an expert in pearls, which were imported from the Persian Gulf region. Apart from the diamonds, Mir Jumla's territories in Karnataka were abundant in bezoars, iron, steel and saltpetre.[15]

Both Jumla and Tavernier immediately hit it off during their first encounter and forged a deep friendship that proved to be mutually beneficial. This partnership brought substantial gains to Jumla's business endeavours, while Tavernier gained easy access to previously restricted areas of the mine. Tavernier, intending to sell Persian pearls to the sultan, had to first seek Mir Jumla's recommendation. Their close relationship was documented in Jumla's book, *Les Six Voyages de J. B. Tavernier,* where he once described Tavernier as 'one of the greatest captains who had ever migrated from Persia to India'.

A diamond mine in the Golconda region (1725), from the collection of Pieter van der Aa, a Dutch publisher known for preparing maps and atlases.[16]

Jumla later demonstrated mastery in both military strategy and administration. In contemporary Mughal, English and Deccan circles, he was referred to as 'the chief governor under the king who governed the whole kingdom'.[17]

Tavernier was consistently impressed by various facets of Jumla's character. On one occasion, he witnessed Jumla impart swift and severe Islamic justice. One robber received the punishment of having his stomach ripped open and being left by the side of the highway to endure a painful death. Another thief had his hands and feet amputated. Tavernier also admired the unique postal system devised by Jumla. He provided a detailed description of the system:

> At every two leagues there are small huts, where two or three men employed for running live and immediately when the carrier of a letter has arrived at one of these huts, he throws it to the others at the entrance and one of them takes it up and at once sets off of run. It is

considered unlucky to give a letter into the hand of the messenger; it is therefore thrown at his feet, and he must lift it up.' The runner-post system, being faster than rider post, helped quick transmission of news.[18]

Jumla's rapid ascent stirred jealousy among other courtiers, who sought ways to undermine him and remove him from the kingdom. Despite the risks, he engaged in a scandalous affair with the queen of Golconda, boldly gifting her a four-story palace named Hayat Mahal along with a golden bed weighing 480 kg, adorned with assorted gems and diamonds. His happiness, however, was short-lived, and his downfall came swiftly, ironically on the very bed he had gifted. Recognizing the gravity of his situation, he made the calculated decision to depart, taking the Kohinoor with him, in pursuits of greener pastures of Delhi.

Tavernier Goes to Burma

Meanwhile, Tavernier expressed his desire to purchase rubies from Ava and Dagon in Myanmar and requested that Jumla provide armed guards for the journey. In exchange, Jumla was granted the privilege of being the first buyer of the rubies. The expedition commenced on 1 June 1653, departing from Machilipatnam and arriving in Pegu two weeks later. At the time, the king was away on a tour, leaving his brother as acting governor, who initially displayed hostility. The presence of the Portuguese, already there, added tension as they attempted to turn the governor against the French travellers. However, the situation improved when Tavernier presented the governor with a sizable diamond. This gesture significantly thawed relations, and Tavernier was subsequently treated as a state guest, enjoying the finest food and beverages for a month until the king's return. Upon the king's arrival, another substantial diamond was gifted, and he savoured the Shiraz wine brought from Persia by the traveller.

The Machilipatnam port in 1676, a prime port of Golconda Sultanate.[19]

After three months without any work, Tavernier was eager to visit the Mogok ruby mines, renowned for the world's finest rubies. The journey to the mines was fraught with danger due to marauding robbers. To mitigate the risks, the king provided Tavernier with a substantial number of armed soldiers. The king's foresight proved accurate when the travelling party was attacked, resulting in several casualties. Nonetheless, the journey proved highly lucrative for Tavernier, as he returned with a substantial stock of rubies and sapphires. Additionally, the king bestowed upon him a significant ruby from his royal collection.

Upon returning to India, Tavernier met Mir Jumla as promised and showed him his acquisitions, which left the latter quite astonished. Jumla's gaze was fixed on the biggest and finest ruby, for which the Frenchman demanded the price of one hundred diamonds of the same size and purity. Initially taken aback by the price, Jumla regained his composure and offered Tavernier a hundred diamonds in return. These gems were looted from a Hindu raja of the south. The acquired wealth of at least one hundred generations changed hands in a stroke. Soon, it departed the shores of the country for display and admiration in foreign museums.

In December 1653, Tavernier arrived in Surat in a lavish, gem-studded palanquin with 100 armed men providing security and 200 animals carrying his immense wealth. The palanquin had also been looted from the same Hindu raja. Though Tavernier intended to return to France via land through Persia to trade his gems, the war at Kandhar between the Mughals and Persians thwarted his plans. Furthermore, he found himself amidst small skirmishes between the Dutch and English, adding to his discomfort. Taking a significant risk, he boarded a Dutch ship from a large fleet bound for Persia. Shortly after boarding, English ships intercepted the Dutch, leading to intense firing between the two. Ultimately, many English ships sank, and the Dutch emerged victorious. However, Tavernier continued to face numerous travel hazards before finally reaching France in 1655.

Fifth Voyage

In 1657, Tavernier embarked on his journey to India once again, this time aboard a Dutch ship after taking a few years' rest. He arrived at Smyrna, Greece, and then travelled by caravan to Isfahan, Persia. There, he learned of Aurangzeb's war against his father and brothers for the Mughal throne. India was engulfed in civil strife, with those perceived to be on the wrong side facing merciless executions. Recognizing the danger, Tavernier decided it was wise to remain in Persia until the situation in India stabilized. However, he remained productive, continually seeking out valuable jewels. He sent some of these jewels as gifts to Shaista Khan, general and the subahdar of Bengal, intending to receive repayment in the coming months.

Tavernier buying diamonds from local miners.[20]

Sometime later, in 1659, Tavernier reached Surat but was detained
there by Governor Mirza Arab on the instructions of Aurangzeb.
As months passed without any sign of freedom, he wrote a letter
to Shaista Khan, seeking his assistance in securing his release.
Khan intervened, and Tavernier was freed within a matter of days.
Tavernier once again visited Golconda to buy more exotic gems
before returning to Surat in 1661 and subsequently travelling to
Persia.

Upon his return home, at the age of fifty-six, Tavernier
married Madeline Goisse in 1662. Madeline was the daughter
of Jean Goisse, a jeweller with whom Tavernier had a business
relationship.

Sixth Voyage

By this time, Tavernier had accumulated considerable wealth and had become one of the richest people in France. Eager to settle down and enjoy his riches, he first needed to conclude his affairs in India and elsewhere. Thus, in November 1663, he embarked on his final voyage with his stock of precious stones valued at 400,000 livres (£30,000) or Rs 30 crore in today's currency. Arriving at the palace of King Shah Abbas II of Persia in November 1664, Tavernier showed his possessions to the king, who had a penchant for collecting rare curios. Impressed by the quality of the gems, the king purchased much of Tavernier's merchandise at the price he demanded.

Pleased with the successful sale of his merchandize, Tavernier departed for India in February 1665 and reached Surat a few months later. However, he encountered a setback when a Dutch individual robbed him of a parcel of letters. These letters were entrusted to him to be delivered to the British at the start of his journey and supposedly contained vital information about the outbreak of war in Europe. Despite Tavernier's explanations, the British doubted his story and threatened him with death. Infuriated by this experience, Tavernier wrote a scathing account of the incident in *The History of the Conduct of the Dutch in Asia*.

Once again, the governor told Tavernier that Aurangzeb wanted to inspect the jewels personally. Aware of the Mughal king's temperament and cruelty, especially towards the 'kafirs', Tavernier had no option but to comply with the orders. He travelled through Burhanpur, Sironj, Gwalior and Agra, finally arriving at Jahanabad in September 1665. There, he presented the gems, valued at 23,187 livres, to the Mughal king.

Zafar Khan, the king's uncle, expressed interest in purchasing a particular fancy pearl, albeit at a significantly reduced price.

Politely declining the offer, Tavernier proceeded to meet his dear friend Shaista Khan in Bengal. Khan had been transferred there after the humiliating incident with Aurangzeb when Shivaji cut his fingers. As a token of appreciation for Khan's assistance, Tavernier gifted him some gems.

From there, Tavernier proceeded to Qasim Bazar to collect payment for the goods he had sold. By that time, the Dutch had established factories in the area, and Van Wachtendonk, the director of all Dutch factories in Bengal, warmly welcomed him. After that, Tavernier visited the Mughal office to request payment. However, he received less than expected, as instructed by Zafar Khan, who was displeased with Tavernier for not selling him the pearl. Although Tavernier felt frustrated by this unfair treatment, he was unable to take any action against it.

He travelled to Golconda to purchase gems, and this time he struck gold. Among the gems he acquired, one stood out – a rough-cut, triangle-shaped diamond of the most intense blue hue. Weighing in at 116 carats, it surpassed anything Tavernier had acquired thus far. Many rumours circulated regarding its procurement. Some even speculated that it was once the eye of Sita Mata in a Golconda temple, which had been allegedly gouged out by a thief from whom Tavernier bought it.[21]

He was confident that the French king would be pleased, and he believed that no further voyages would be required henceforth. True to his prediction, the diamond indeed caused a sensation in France and was christened 'Tavernier Blue'. People were astounded by this enormous size and rich blue colour.

In early 1667, Tavernier left Surat for good. After spending some time in Isfahan and Constantinople, he reached Paris in December 1668 to reunite with his family and enjoy some well-deserved rest.

The Journey of a Billion-year-old Gem to Foreign Shores

Tavernier Blue, like others, is fundamentally a biopsy of Mother Earth. Approximately 150 km below the earth's surface, tonnes of pressure and temperature reaching thousands of degrees forced the carbon to crystallize. The volcanoes on India's Deccan plateau brought these gems vertically to the surface of the Krishna River's delta, where they were mined centuries ago. Now, it was embarking on a new horizontal journey to foreign shores, where its pristine beauty would be altered.

King Louis XIV hired a court jeweller in 1675 to rework and set the exquisite blue diamond in a gold cravat.[22]

Tavernier had gained considerable fame in his home country for his exploits in the East, particularly in India. King Louis XIV of France invited him to his palace, and showcasing his skills in selling gems, Tavernier sold him a significant quantity, including, by conservative estimates, 147 kg of pure gold. As a token of appreciation, Tavernier was granted the title of a noble along with a substantial payment, further enriching him.

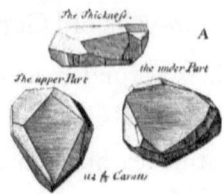

Tavernier's original sketch of the Tavernier Blue.[23]

Louis XIV, much like our Mohammed Shah 'Rangila', was vain and deeply immersed in debauchery. Unlike other European kings, he considered himself a representative of God. Dubbing himself the 'Sun King', 'Roi-Soleil', he even adopted the emblem of the sun. To convey the idea of his reign as the epitome of enlightenment, he adorned his palace in Versailles with luminous chandeliers, making it brilliantly lit. The acquisition of various diamonds from India was part of this effort, symbolizing enlightenment and grandeur.

Among the gems purchased by the king was the Tavernier Blue. However, he was dissatisfied with some of its rough edges and impurities in the middle. He instructed the royal jeweller to smooth it out, which was done, albeit resulting in a reduced size of 69 carats. Nevertheless, the diamond still glimmered, impressing the king when it was set into his cravat pin. From then on, it became known as the Blue Diamond of the Crown of France, or simply the 'French Blue'.

The depravity continued and reached such a point that Louis XIV's descendant, Louis XVI, faced massive public protests as the royal treasury emptied and the people suffered from famine. Louis XVI had a more famous wife, Marie Antoinette, who infamously remarked that the citizens should 'eat cake if they could not afford the bread'. During the French Revolution in 1792–93, Louis XVI and his wife were imprisoned and executed. Amidst the chaos of the revolution, the French Blue mysteriously disappeared, likely looted by marauding groups. When Napoleon became the king of France, he tried to recover all the crown jewels, including the French Blue, but was unsuccessful.

The transformation of the Hope Diamond over the years.[24]

Later, in 1812, the stone reappeared in London, now weighing only 45.52 carats, when it was purchased by British King George IV. By 1830, the royal family faced considerable debt and sold the diamond to London-based banker and financier Thomas Hope, who renamed it the 'Hope Diamond'. Unfortunately, the cutting of the diamond was described as a 'butchered job', as it reduced the diamond by 23.5 carats and significantly diminished its 'extraordinary lustre'.

In between, the diamond also passed through the hands of renowned French jeweller Pierre Cartier and Evalyn Walsh McLean, one of the richest Americans. Later, it came into the possession of the famous London-based jeweller Harry Winston. George Switzer, an American mineralogist working at the Smithsonian Institution in Washington, DC, advocated for the gem to be displayed for all visitors in the museum. Despite initial reluctance, Winston decided to donate it and sent it by regular post from England to the US in 1958, where it found its permanent home in the National Museum of Natural History, Washington. Thus, a billion-year-old diamond now resides in the museum, having travelled a great deal through time and space, detached from its Hindu history.

Curse of the Hope

Like other valuable diamonds, the Hope Diamond had a perceived curse associated with it, whether imaginary or real. It was often likened to the curse of Tutankhamun, where it was said that anyone who disturbed the mummy of the ancient Egyptian pharaoh would be cursed. The Hope Diamond, considered by some to be a blood diamond due to the many deaths associated with it, had a dark history.

Unconfirmed reports suggests that Tavernier met a grim fate, allegedly mauled by a pack of wild dogs. Louis XVI, the first known 'owner' of the diamond, met his demise when he was hanged during the French Revolution. The subsequent owner, British King George IV, also faced financial ruin, despite the height of colonialism. Afterwards, even the wealthy Hope family, one of the richest in England, lost much of their wealth due to bad investments and were compelled to sell off many of their assets. Against the advice of their well-wishers, they chose to retain the diamond. However, their descendant Francis Hope eventually had to sell it to New York-based jeweller Joseph Frankel's Sons & Company in 1901 to settle his debts. Just a few years later, in 1907, a major recession stuck the US, leading to the closure of the company, while banks of similar stature remained operational.

Some individuals capitalized on the perceived curse to enhance the diamond's mystique and sales appeal. Pierre Cartier, inspired by the theme of the novel *The Moonstone* by English author Wilkie Collins, saw an opportunity. The novel, echoing the real-life saga of a large gem akin to the Kohinoor, looted by Muslim invaders and believed to have invited the wrath of Hindu gods, struck a chord. According to legend, misfortune befell the foreigners until the gem was returned to its designated place of worship. Cartier embellished the story and presented it to Evalyn McLean, a scion of one of the wealthiest American families, in 1910. Intrigued by the mysterious stone, she purchased it at an exorbitant price and started flaunting, inadvertently attracting the 'evil eye'. Tragedy befell McLean when her ten-year-old son, Vinson, was killed in a road accident. American tabloids were rife with conspiracy theories, suggesting that a curse had brought misfortune upon her. According to these sensational accounts, evil rays were unleashed when the sacred diamond was cut. The calamity continued to afflict McLean, as her husband, Ned McLean, succumbed to insanity when he became bankrupt. To settle his debts, many of his companies had to be liquidated. In a tragic turn of events, her daughter committed suicide in 1946, further fuelling the belief in the malevolent curse. In light of these tragedies, her family made the decision to sell the diamond to Winston.

Later, James Todd, the postman who delivered Winston's package to the Smithsonian, experienced a series of misfortunes. His wife and dog passed away, he suffered a leg injury in an accident and his home was destroyed by fire.

As recently as 1995, the prestigious *Life* magazine published an article delving into the origins of the curse of the Hope Diamond:

> In all but the brightest light it smolders like a huge sullen eye.... The jewel, so the story goes, was once the eye of a Hindu idol Rama Sita. When it was stolen, Ram cursed everyone who would come to possess the stone. Indeed, fate has not been kind to those who have owned the eye of the god.[25]

Richard Kurin, the author of *Hope Diamond: The Legendary History of a Cursed Gem*, presents an interesting theory that these diamonds came to be perceived as 'cursed' due to the methods through which they were acquired. He states, 'When the powerful take things from the less powerful, the powerless don't have much to do except curse the powerful.'[26]

What Happened to Owners and Wearers of the Gem[27]			
Date acquired	Owner	Fate	Notes
Acquired the diamond between 1640 and 1667, possibly 1653	Jean-Baptiste Tavernier	Died at the age of eighty-four	
1668	Louis XIV of France	Died at the age of seventy-six	
1722	Louis XV of France	Died at the age of sixty-four	
1775	Louis XVI of France	Guillotined at the age of thirty-eight	
1775	Marie Antoinette	Guillotined at the age of thirty-seven	Wife of Louis XVI
1805	King George IV of the United Kingdom	Died at the age of sixty-seven	Doubtful whether he ever owned it
1812	Daniel Eliason, a London jeweller	Died at the age of seventy-one	
1830	Thomas Hope	Died at the age of sixty-two	
1839	Henry Philip Hope		
1861	Henry Pelham-Clinton, sixth Duke of Newcastle	Died at the age of forty-five	

1884	Lord Francis Hope	Suffered bankruptcy and died at the age of seventy-five	
1894	May Yohé	Died poor at the age of seventy-two	Wife of Lord Francis Hope
1901	Adolph Weil, London jewel merchant		
1901	Simon Frankel		
1908	Selim Habib		Possibly as agent for Turkish Sultan Hamid
1908	Sultan Abdul Hamid II of Turkey	Deposed in 1909 and died at the age of seventy-five	Disputed whether the Sultan ever owned it
1909	Simon Rosenau		
1910	Pierre Cartier	Died at the age of eighty-six	
1911	Edward Beale McLean and Evalyn Walsh McLean	The couple divorced in 1932. Edward suffered mental illness and died at the age of fifty-one or fifty-two; Evalyn died at the age of sixty from pneumonia	Jeweller who gave it to Smithsonian 1958
1947	Harry Winston	Died at the age of eighty-three	
1958	The Smithsonian Institution	Prospered and the attendance went up	

Changes in Hope Diamond Over Time[28]			
Date acquired	Owner	Changes in the diamond	Value when sold
1653	Jean-Baptiste Tavernier	116 metric carats	220,000 livres; he also received Patent of Nobility worth 450,000 livres
1668	Louis XIV of France	Triangular 69 metric-carat gem set on a cravat pin	After his death, given to his son
1715	Louis XV of France	Set into a pendant, Order of Golden Fleece	After his death, given to his son
1775	Louis XVI of France	69 metric carats	Stolen
1812	Daniel Eliason, a London based jeweller	About 44 carats	$65,000
1812–30	George IV of UK		Sold to pay off king's debts after death
1830 to 1839	Henry Hope (1774–1839)	Came to be known as the 'Hope Diamond'	After his death, given to his son
1839	Henry Thomas Hope		After his death, given to his son
1861	Henry Pelham-Clinton, Duke of Newcastle		After his death, given to his son
1884	Francis Hope		$250,000
1894	May Yohé, wife of Henry Hope		£29,000 (£2,484,530 as of 2011)
1901	Adolph Weil, London jeweller		$141,032

1908	Sultan Abdul Hamid (Disputed whether he ever owned it)	44 3/8 carats	$80,000
1910	Pierre Cartier	Reset on a three-tiered circlet of large white diamonds on a pendant to appeal to Evalyn McLean	$200K; various estimates
1911	Edward McLean & Evalyn McLean	44.5 carats	$180,000
1947	Harry Winston, a New York jeweller	The bottom of the diamond was recut to increase brilliance	He bought the whole McLean collection and put it up for exhibition in various US cities
1958	Smithsonian Institution	45.52 carats in 1974	$250 million (current value)

Tavernier's Description of the Indian Conditions

In his book, Tavernier describes the prevailing conditions in India, especially during Aurangzeb's era, when he spent the most time in India. His detailed accounts have earned him recognition as an authority on that period. Tavernier was in India during the zenith of the Mughal Empire under Shah Jahan, who was estimated to possess around 23 per cent of world's GDP during his reign and is often considered the wealthiest Indian in history. Under Shah Jahan's rule, in 1690 BCE, India's annual GDP was $450 million (Rs 288 crore), surpassing that of France by tenfold.

European traders, including Tavernier, reported that Shah Jahan possessed over half a million carats of unmounted emeralds in his treasury, many of which were acquired from or gifted by the Portuguese. Tavernier's last voyage concluded just two months after Aurangzeb ascended the throne. Tavernier observed that Aurangzeb displayed extreme barbarism and relentless invasions against Hindu kingdoms.

He further writes about the king:

> To him the Deccan was Dar-al Harb: he determined to make it Dar-al-Islam. Religion induced Aurangzib to abjure the pleasures of the senses as completely as if he had indeed become the fakir he had once desired to be. No animal food passed his lips, and his drink was water; so that, as Tavernier says, he became thin and meagre, to which the great fasts which he keeps have contributed. During the whole of the duration of the comet [four weeks, in 1665], which appeared very large in India, where I then was, Aurangzib only drank a little water and ate a small quantity of millet bread; this so much affected his health that he nearly died, for besides this he slept on the ground, with only a tiger's skin over him; and since that time he has never had perfect health.[29]

Earlier, Tavernier witnessed the construction of the Taj Mahal, where 20,000 workers toiled continuously to give it its pristine finish:

> The Taj Mahal was finished in 1648, nearly eighteen years after the death of the queen, who was interred, meanwhile, in a tomb in the garden. Tavernier saw it, while it was being built, and says that twenty thousand workmen were continuously employed.[30]

Tavernier also expressed strong opinions about Mughal paintings, suggesting they were highly influenced by European Christian paintings, especially those from Italy. He noted the significant impact of Jesuit missions in Agra and other cities on the development of Indian painting. Jahangir, described as 'very fond of pictures and an excellent judge of them', is said to have kept a picture of the Madonna behind a curtain, as depicted in a contemporary painting that has fortunately been preserved.

Tavernier observed a representation of Jahangir's tomb on a gate outside Agra, which was 'carved with a great black pall with many torches of white wax, and two Jesuit Fathers at the end'. He mentioned that Shah Jahan allowed this to remain because 'his father and himself had learned some principles of mathematics and astrology from the Jesuits'.[31]

The Augustinian Manrique, who travelled to India during the reign of Shah Jahan, also observed that a palace in Lahore was decorated with images of Christian saints. In many Mughal portraits, the emperor's head is depicted surrounded by an aureole or nimbus, and various other elements in the Agra and Delhi schools of painting bear resemblance to contemporary Italian art.[32]

Tavernier also documented the Kohinoor, which was held by his friend, Mir Jumla, for numerous years. When Jumla's relationship with the nizam soured, Jumla appealed to Shah Jahan to attack the Deccan and usurp all its riches. As part of his entreaty, he presented the Kohinoor to Shah Jahan, who was indeed delighted to receive such a remarkable and priceless jewel. In response, the Mughal king dispatched his son, Prince Aurangzeb, to invade the nizam's territory.

During his sixth voyage, Aurangzeb summoned Tavernier to Delhi to inspect and purchase his jewels. During his visit, Tavernier beheld the magnificence of the peacock throne upon which the king was seated. The throne was rectangular in shape, crafted from 150 kg of solid gold and adorned with 230 kg of precious stones. It stood on four legs, with its canopy supported by twelve columns. Two peacocks adorned each side of the throne, hence the name. Commissioned by Shah Jahan on 22 March 1635, it was studded with numerous balas rubies, emeralds, pearls, diamonds and other precious stones.

Tavernier meticulously noted the intricate details of the throne, counting 108 large balas rubies, all cabochon-cut, with weights ranging from about 100 carats to over 200 carats. Additionally, he observed 116 large emeralds adorning the throne, all exhibiting excellent colour but many displaying flaws, a common feature of emeralds. The smallest one weighed about 30 carats and the largest about 60 carats. The cost of the peacock throne amounted to twice the construction expenses of the Taj Mahal, underscoring its unparalleled opulence. If it were intact today, its value would be estimated at around Rs 550 crore.

One of Shah Jahan's titles, 'Zille-I-Illahi', meaning 'Shadow of God on Earth', was aptly reflected in the creation of the throne, which symbolized the paradise on earth within his palaces in Agra and Delhi. Modelled after the legendary throne of Solomon, a mythical Biblical Jewish king, it was venerated even within Islamic circles despite its Biblical inspiration.

Tavernier also extensively described how Muslims tortured Hindus at every turn, killed them and desecrated their temples at will. He was surprised at how readily Hindus submitted to Muslims but was able to correctly identify the cause. He observed:

> The Idolaters among the Indians are so numerous, that they are reckon'd to be five or six for one Mahometan. It seems a wonderful thing, that such a prodigious multitude of men should be cow'd by a handful, and bow so easily under the yoak of the Mahometan Princes. *But that wonder well may cease, when we consider that those Idolaters are not in union among themselves; for Superstition has introduc'd such a diversity of Opinions and Customs, that they can never agree one with another.*[33] [Emphasis added]

There was a village called Gandikota with a strategic fort atop a hill in the heart of Golconda. After the raw diamonds were mined from Golconda, they were stored in the fort before being transported to Europe, where the technology to cut and polish them had been developed, enhancing their sparkle and brilliance. The fort was under the control of Hindu raja Timma Nayar, prompting the Golconda sultan to covet it and assign Mir Jumla to capture it in 1650. Despite months of siege, the fort resisted surrender. On the contrary, Jumla suffered heavy losses among his troops due to gunfire and diseases. Resorting to deception, Jumla befriended a French gunner employed by Hindus and offered him and his colleagues four times their monthly pay, along with some diamonds. The result was now foregone.[34] Later, the nawab aimed to install canons there, considering its tactical position. The project needed a substantial amount of copper. According to Tavernier:

> There is in Gandikot a pagoda (temple) which is considered to be one of the principal in India, where there are many idols, some being of gold and others of silver. Among these idols there were six of copper, three of which were seated on their heels, and the three others were about 10 feet high. After Maille, a French, had made all preparations to melt these metals and the idols which had been brought from different places, he accomplished the melting of all except the six large idols of the famous pagoda of Gandikot. It was impossible for him to melt them, no matter how much the Nawab expended; and he even threatened the priests of the pagoda, whom he accused of having bewitched the idols. In short, Maille never accomplished making a single cannon, one being split, another incomplete.[35]

Jumla, like many other Muslims, was always keen to destroy temples. In Poonamalle, located in present-day Tamil Nadu, he destroyed a famous temple and erected a mosque over it in 1653, during the reign of Abdullah Qutb Shah of Golconda. He plundered numerous gems from the idols and later sold them to the highest bidder, with Tavernier being among them.[36]

Due to relentless cruelty, many Hindus chose to convert. Tavernier observed that some Hindus converted because they felt that after conversion, they would be relieved from the necessity of labour. He further observed that the Mughals employed Persians to prominent positions, while native Muslims were relegated to less significant roles, with Hindus faring the worst in this unjust scheme of things.[37]

Sadhus near a temple, as illustrated by Tavernier.[38]

Even though Tavernier built his career in India and acquired the finest diamonds and gemstones, he harboured deep animosity towards Hindus, their culture, customs and their idols. He considered them worse than Jews, placing them at the bottom of the social hierarchy. He preferred dealing with Christians first, followed by Muslims. Here are some examples of his observations regarding Hindu deities:

> After having travelled 3 leagues on the other side of the river, we found a great pagoda built on a platform to which one ascended by fifteen or twenty steps. There was an image there of a cow in black marble, and numerous idols of 4 or 5 feet in height, which were all deformed, one having many heads, another many arms and many legs, another many horns, and the most hideous are the most adored and receive most offerings.[39]

He was also astonished by the custom of bringing water from the holy rivers, especially the Ganga, to their native villages. Countless people embarked on long journeys, walking hundreds of miles along the roads to accomplish this task, sometimes selling the water along the way. He noted:

Ganges water is often given at weddings, 'each guest receiving a cup or two, according to the liberality of the host, sometimes 2,000 or 3,000 rupees' worth of it is consumed at a wedding'.[40]

However, he appeared to understand that all these deities are manifestations of a single God:

Though the Idolatrous Indians attribute to the Creature, as to Cows, Apes, and several Monsters, those Divine Honours which are only due to the true Deity; yet they acknowledg one only Infinite God, Almighty, and only Wise, the Creator of Heaven and Earth, who fills all places with his presence. They call him in some places Permesser.[41]

His Retired Life

In April 1670, he purchased a sprawling castle in Aubonne, near Geneva. He restored and Orientalized the castle in Persian aesthetic, and it was here that he proceeded to write his magnum opus, *The Six Voyages*. Published in 1676, it went one to become a smash hit in Europe. However, the book is surrounded by several controversies. First, Tavernier was not considered an intellectual and even lacked formal education. He enlisted the help of a ghostwriter, with whom his relationship soured, resulting in numerous factual errors in the account. However, this does not detract from the interesting stories swirling around him, his journey and the destinations he visited. He remained an indefatigable traveller and died while travelling to Russia in 1689, allegedly attacked by a pack of dogs.

Epilogue

One can't help but marvel at Tavernier's courage and fortune, as he traversed through Mughal, Dutch and English territories in India unscathed. He dedicated approximately forty years, nearly half of his active life, to exploring far-flung countries despite the significant risks involved. His journeys often lasted for weeks or even months, using various modes of transportation such as horses, walking, mules, wagons and boats. He was fond of Persian Shiraz wine and always carried a few bottles with him, often presenting them to kings and sultans.

Despite carrying precious gems and diamonds, Tavernier was rarely robbed or attacked, a testament to his patience, exceptional organizational skills and robust security measures. Ensuring the safe transportation of such valuable goods and arranging suitable accommodations for various stopovers demanded considerable time and effort.

However, Tavernier's impact on India was detrimental, as he depleted the land of many of its diamonds, a trend continued by Islamic and British invaders. Today, except for the Jacob diamond, few large diamonds remain in India. Nehru, despite his numerous achievements, rejected any claim for the 'ghar-wapasi' of the Kohinoor, famously stating, 'Diamonds are for the Emperors and India does not need Emperors.'[42] India has made some faint requests for the return of the Kohinoor, while for others, it hasn't pursued the matter. In contrast, France continues to assert ownership over the Hope Diamond.

Indeed, diamonds may be forever, but for India, they seem to be lost to the sands of time.

7

Mark Twain

'India has two million gods, and worships them all. In religion other countries are paupers; India is the only millionaire.'

—Mark Twain

Samuel Langhorne Clemens (1835–1910), with the pen name of Mark Twain, was an American author and humourist celebrated for his literary contributions that left an indelible mark on American literature. Renowned for his literary works that captured the essence of American society, Twain has written groundbreaking novels such as *The Adventures of Tom Sawyer* (1876) and its sequel, *The Adventures of Huckleberry Finn* (1884). The latter is frequently referred to as the 'Great American Novel', and Mark Twain is often hailed as the greatest humourist the United States has ever produced, with some even dubbing him 'the father of American literature'.

Mark Twain[1]

Twain was a wealthy man but became insolvent after investing heavily in some promising yet failed startup ventures. In 1896, at the age of sixty-one, Mark Twain set sail on a world tour within the English-speaking British Empire. The primary purpose of his journey was to alleviate financial burdens resulting from failed investments and business ventures. One such project was the Paige Compositor, an invention intended to replace the human typesetter – an innovative concept 130 years ago.

India was one of the destinations on his itinerary, reflecting the growing interest of Western intellectuals in the mystique and allure of the East. Accompanied by his wife Olivia and daughter Clara, he spent three months in India, keenly observing its everyday life with both enthusiasm and critique. In the process, he became the first prominent American to visit India. This sojourn is not as well-documented as some of his other travels, but it nonetheless adds a fascinating chapter to Twain's adventures.

Twain arrived in Bombay and proceeded to tour several cities, including Allahabad, Lucknow, Calcutta and Varanasi. He had gained substantial popularity in English-speaking regions, attracting an audience of at least 55,000 British stationed in India, eager to absorb Twain's intellectual insights. Additionally, there were several Westernized rich Indians who sought to attend his talks and lectures for social recognition.

As mentioned earlier, his observations of Indian society and culture during this trip were not as extensively recorded as his experiences in other parts of the world. However, he did share some reflections on India in his travelogue, *Following the Equator*, (1897), which chronicled his global journey. In his book, Twain touched upon various aspects of Indian life, including the majestic landscapes, the complex social fabric and the British colonial presence. He remarked on the intricacies of Hinduism and the caste system, providing a glimpse into his perceptions of

Indian society. During his journey in India, Twain encountered the country's diversity, from the bustling cities to the serene landscapes along the Ganges.

Twain was born in Missouri, a state rampant with slavery, and grew up witnessing the cruel treatment of Africans by white Christians in his homeland. This experience resurfaced during his travels in India, where he observed similar mistreatment of Indians by the British. His travels in India had a profound impact on him, and two years later, he wrote, 'How I did loathe that journey around the world – except the sea part and India.' Initially an imperialist who strongly supported the American government's invasion of the Hawaiian Islands, Twain's perspective began to shift, likely influenced by the harsh and inhuman conditions he witnessed in India. By the 1890s, he had become anti-imperialist. When the US invaded, captured and annexed the Philippines in 1899, Twain vehemently protested against such actions. The Philippines underwent a similar process to India, eventually gaining independence in 1946.

Twain in India

Twain left Colombo and landed in Bombay in 1896, where he lodged at the prestigious Watson's Hotel in the upscale Kala Ghoda area. It was from the balcony of his room here that he observed the city's crows, a famous chapter in his book, *Following the Equator*. The hotel was not only the most renowned establishment in the city but also the first venue in India to screen the Lumière Brothers' Cinematographe invention in 1896. It's said that Indian industrialist Jamshed Tata was barred from attending the screening due to his 'Indian' heritage, which inspired him to retaliate by constructing the iconic Taj Mahal Hotel.

The Watson's was probably the oldest surviving four-story, fully cast-iron-framed building in the world. Equipped with electric lights that stayed illuminated until midnight, it offered quite a luxury for its time. Twain observed that it took seventeen porters to transport their modest luggage to their upstairs rooms, as the hotel lift was out of order. Astonishingly, two porters were needed to carry a cigar tin and an umbrella. However, Twain was shocked by the demeaning behaviour of the hotel's German manager, who resorted to slapping the porters even for minor errors, evoking memories of the treatment of African slaves back home.

As a celebrated author, Twain had the opportunity to meet with all the powerful figures of his time. He met Lord Sandhurst, the governor of Bombay, at his opulent, expansive bungalow in Malabar Hills. Twain expressed his reservations about the brutal treatment inflicted on Indians by the British. However, the governor was unimpressed by such impractical observations and instead started enumerating the benefits of hospitals, railways, schools, universities, telegraphs and efficient administration that the British had brought to impoverished and 'beastly' India. Twain also wondered how merely 55,000 British individuals had subjugated 10 crore Indians for over 200 years.

'And might there be more of my sort where I came from, and when would they be hanged – and so on, until I could no longer endure the embarrassment of it.' An excerpt about Twain's conversations with crows in Bombay.[2]

While in Bombay, Twain visited the Tower of Silence (dakhma), a unique cremation ground for Parsis, where their deceased are placed for transition to heaven. Bodies are left exposed in the tower to attract vultures for consumption. Purity is a fundamental principle governing Parsee funerals, similar to Hindu customs. According to Zoroastrian beliefs, the elements, earth, fire and water, are sacred and must not be contaminated by contact with the deceased. Hence, bodies cannot be cremated or buried; instead, they are entrusted to designated funeral executives at the tower, inaccessible to others. Within hours, vultures strip the flesh from the skeleton, leaving behind only bones.

Early 20th-century drawing of the dakhma on Malabar Hill, Bombay.[3]

The Parsees claim that their method of disposing of the deceased provides effective protection for the living. They argue that it prevents the spread of corruption, impurities of any kind or disease germs, as no cloth or garment that has come into contact with the deceased is allowed to touch the living thereafter. They maintain that nothing harmful to the outside world proceeds from the Towers of Silence.[4]

Though Twain's stay in Bombay was brief, he fully immersed himself in the vibrant colours, rich scents and captivating sights of India. His words capture this experience eloquently:

> This is indeed India! the land of dreams and romance, of fabulous wealth and fabulous poverty, of splendor and rags, of palaces and hovels, of famine and pestilence, of genii and giants and Aladdin lamps, of tigers and elephants, the cobra and the jungle, the country of hundred nations and a hundred tongues, of a thousand religions and two million gods, cradle of the human race, birthplace of human speech, mother of history, grandmother of legend, great-grandmother of tradition, whose yesterdays bear date with the mouldering antiquities of the rest of the nations – the one sole country under the sun that is endowed with an imperishable interest for alien prince and alien peasant, for lettered and ignorant, wise and fool, rich and poor, bond and free, the one land that all men desire to see, and having seen once, by even a glimpse, would not give that glimpse for the shows of all the rest of the globe combined.[5]

From Bombay, Twain journeyed to Calcutta, the then-capital of India, arriving after a week's travel. Lord Elgin, a Scot, wielded absolute authority over the vast country with a no-nonsense approach. Twain keenly observed the intricacies of Indian life. He received an invitation to attend a session of the Supreme Legislative Council, an event exclusive to provincial governors and Indian princes. The native princes were seated according to their status, determined by the number of gun salutes they were entitled to. When a maharaja of higher rank unexpectedly showed up, everyone had to stand up and rearrange their seating according to his superior status.

Despite his keen powers of observation, Twain could not resist drawing comparisons between India and the Arab world. For many Europeans and Americans, the Middle East served as the standard – it was either Jerusalem or Mecca. An Indian night inevitably drew comparisons to an Arabian night. Indians were often perceived as lowly natives, either to be pitied or scorned. In this way, there seemed to be little difference between Muslim travellers of the medieval age and their modern American and European counterparts.

Darjeeling

Twain described his trip to Darjeeling in great detail, highlighting the unique experience of travelling by toy train, which chugged along at a leisurely 7–8 miles per hour, taking hours to cover just 50 miles. Located approximately 7,000 feet above sea level, Darjeeling served as the summer capital of the Bengal government. The train was vital for many British tea planters who owned lucrative plantations around the hill station, producing approximately 8 million pounds of high-quality tea per year. With a population of 155,000, Darjeeling was designed to evoke the ambiance of a quaint English town nestled in the Himalayas, boasting amenities such as tennis courts, palatial clubs, flourishing English roses, Victorian-style bungalows, a stone clock tower and even Protestant churches. In a nutshell, it was a home away from home.

From the train, Twain observed Gurkhas laboriously carrying huge luggage uphill on the roads for miles. He learned that Gurkhas formed the backbone of the British army and played a significant role in maintaining control over the Indian population. He also witnessed women carrying almost equal loads on their backs, all with seemingly cheerful expressions.

Like many other Europeans of his time, he embarked on a tiger hunt, proudly boasting killing thirteen in a single day. Despite his success, he endured a harrowing encounter when bitten by a deadly cobra during the hunt, miraculously surviving the ordeal. Additionally, he encountered crowds of Buddhists joyfully singing, dancing and spinning prayer wheels, enjoying their lives.

Reflecting on these moments, he experienced brief pangs of guilt for not fully embracing such carefree moments himself.[6]

Twain considered himself lucky to have a clear view of Mount Kanchenjunga, as many tourists often left without catching a glimpse of it as it is always surrounded by clouds. He recounted a joke about a tourist who stayed for twenty-two days but failed to see the mountain. However, upon checking out of the hotel on the final day and seeing the enormous bill, he certainly beheld the tallest thing in the Himalayas![7]

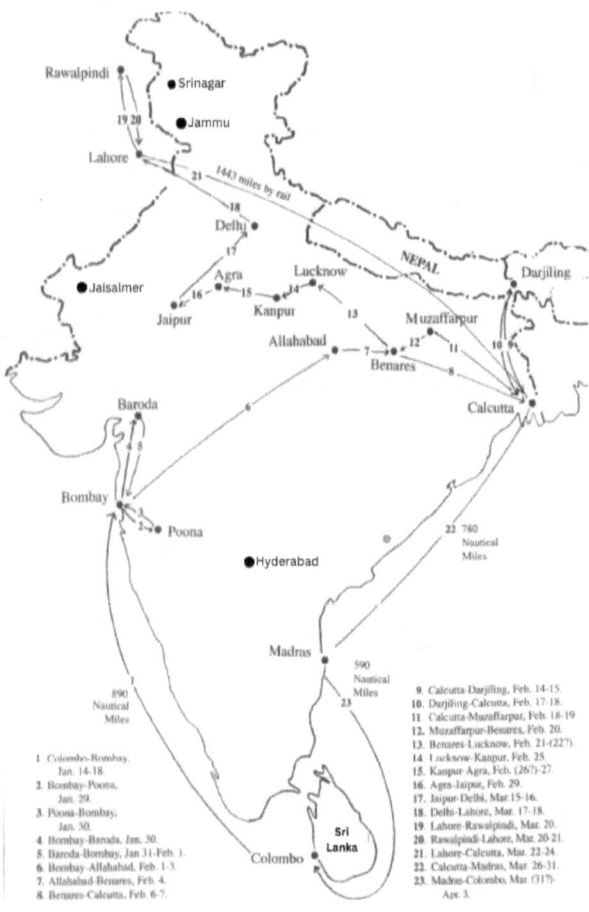

A map detailing the journey of Mark Twain.[8]

Benares

From the Himalayas, Twain proceeded to Benares and underwent a profound transformation. He expressed, 'Benares is older than history, older than tradition, older even than legend, and looks twice as old as all of them put together.... I find that the site of the town was the beginning-place of the Creation.'[9]

However, he did not react favourably to the filth and foul smell of the city, which unfortunately persists even to this date. Like every other Christian and Muslim, converting the native 'unclean' Hindus was always at the back of his mind. He heaved a sigh when he was told that the Baptist Missionary Society, the Church Missionary Society, the London Missionary Society, the Wesleyan Missionary Society and the Zenana Bible and Medical Mission had already opened schools and worked among the children. He further believed that it was challenging to convert adults, and focussing on children yielded the best results.

Twain even quickly did the math regarding converting the teeming Hindus:

I was told by an American missionary that in India there are 640 Protestant missionaries at work. At first it seemed an immense force, but of course that was a thoughtless idea. One missionary to 500,000 natives—no, that is not a force; it is the reverse of it; 640 marching against an intrenched camp of 300,000,000—the odds are too great. A force of 640 in Benares alone would have its hands over-full with 8,000 Brahmin priests for adversary. Missionaries need to be well equipped with hope and confidence, and this equipment they seem to have always had in all parts of the world.[10]

He also seemed to be quite confused about the multitude of Hindu gods and their names:

I should have been glad to acquire some sort of idea of Hindoo theology, but the difficulties were too great, the matter was too intricate. Even the mere A, B, C of it is baffling. There is a trinity

– Brahma, Shiva, and Vishnu – independent powers, apparently, though one cannot feel quite sure of that, because in one of the temples there is an image where an attempt has been made to concentrate the three in one person. The three have other names and plenty of them, and this makes confusion in one's mind. The three have wives and the wives have several names, and this increases the confusion. There are children, the children have many names, and thus the confusion goes on and on ... the lingams in Benares 'outnumber the inhabitants'.... Let a Hindoo regiment be marched through the distinct, and as soon as they cross the line and enter the limits of the holy place, they rend the air with cries of 'Kashi ji ki jai jai'.[11]

Here, he could not openly express his aversion towards pagan Hinduism and instead spoke in a manner that could be construed as outright racist:

One could properly expect an ass to have an aversion to being turned into a Hindoo. One could understand that he could lose dignity by it, also self-respect, and nine-tenths of his intelligence. But the Hindoo changed into an ass wouldn't lose anything, unless you count his religion. And he would gain much release from his slavery to two million gods and twenty million priests, fakeers, holy mendicants, and other sacred bacilli; he would escape the Hindoo hell; he would also escape the Hindoo heaven.[12]

Way back in 1894, he found the Ganga River foul-smelling and dirty. If he were in India today, what would he say when it is even dirtier? He was intrigued to find sewers emptying into the holy river and hundreds of corpses floating around. He was even more surprised to learn that no disease ever broke out due to the purifying properties of the Ganga. He came to know that several British scientists had already tested the waters and found some remarkable elements. He wondered how the Hindus knew all this. In a rare moment of emotional weakness, he stated, 'How did they find out the water's secret in those ancient ages? Had they germ-scientists then? We do not know. We only know that they had a civilization long before we emerged from savagery.'[13]

Twain even witnessed a cremation, which for an aristocratic American, was nothing short of revolting. He wrote in graphic detail about how the body was burned and how the skull was broken. The responsibility of burning the body fell on the eldest son to ensure that the deceased could reach heaven. Consequently, Hindus, he observed, desired sons primarily for this purpose. He was informed that the fire used in the cremation was considered sacred and therefor costly. As people dying in Benares were believed to ascend directly to heaven, everything became more expensive.

He disliked the idols in the city; to him, they were all misshapen and ugly. They seemed omnipresent, even on the ghats, where most were life-size and painted on the walls. The city was essentially a museum of idols. Additionally, there were numerous lingams, prompting him to quip that if Vishnu had foreseen what his town was to become, he might have called it 'Idolville' or 'Lingamburg'.[14]

He felt like a cold, refreshing wind blowing in a hot, stifling and stale atmosphere when he saw a couple of mosques in the city. He praised them fervently, describing them as graceful and inspiring. He likened the minarets to elegant candles and speculated that if Christians 'inherited' them, they would become even more beautiful.

British Rule over India

Otherwise dull and drab, his book comes alive whenever he discusses the British (Christian) subjugation of India (Hindu). Twain recounted story after story portraying the Hindus as cowardly and praising the British leaders as virtuous.

In one particular incident, which Twain fondly narrates, Governor-General Warren Hastings levied a £50,000 fine on the Hindu raja of Benares for a minor indiscretion dating back to 1781.

Despite the raja commanding thousands of soldiers and Hastings having insufficient troops, with too few Indian soldiers and just three white officers, Hastings boldly dispatched his forces to the raja's stronghold. To everyone's surprise, the raja surrendered without attempting resistance. He was subsequently arrested and confined to a room within his own fort. However, there was still a twist in the story.[15]

In their haste, the soldiers forgot to load ammunition into their guns, and upon reaching the raja's fort, they discovered their weapons were empty. When news of the arrest of the raja reached the mob, they swiftly attacked and lynched all the soldiers. Hastings narrowly escaped, fleeing for his life. However, he returned with a full battalion and extracted brutal revenge, killing everyone in the town. Twain continued, emphasizing that on that day, Hastings not only secured the Indian Empire for England but also liberated the Indians themselves, 'those wretched heirs of a hundred centuries of pitiless oppression and abuse'.[16]

Twain observed critically, suggesting that he believed the Indian race was fit for slavery:

> In a quarter of a century, from being nobodies, and feared by none, they become confessed lords and masters, feared by all, sovereigns included, and served by all, sovereigns included. It makes the fairy tales sound true. The English had not been afraid to enlist native soldiers to fight against their own people and keep them obedient.[17]

In the winter months of January and February in north India, Twain still felt hot and found everything dusty and dirty. He believed that the winters in India were warmer than peak summers in America, and mused had he arrived during the summer season, it would have been unbearable, possibly causing his soul to leave his body.

In between, he was told a couple of stories reminiscent of *The Monk Who Sold His Ferrari,* where educated and wealthy people renounced worldly pursuits to seek solitude in the Himalayas. One of them was Swami Bhaskarananda Saraswati, who was expert in Vedanta philosophy and the Sanskrit language and was said to have attained nirvana. Twain even met him on his trip , but he did not write whether he was impressed with him or not. He compared this act to the 'noble' tenets of Christianity. Thus, even during his journey to such an exotic land as India, thoughts of Christianity, conversion and colonialism never left his mind.

Left: The British gasping for air and water in the Black Hole cell.
Right: Guards teasing the prisoners.[18]

Throughout his trip, his first priority was locating memorials of Christians; he diligently searched for them wherever possible. His second priority was Islam, another Abrahamic cousin. Hindus, unfortunately, found themselves at the bottom of the hierarchy, often overlooked. In Calcutta, he sought out the Black Hole memorial to pay his respects to the fallen white European soldiers. The Black Hole of Calcutta was a small prison cell measuring 18-foot by 14-foot with only two small windows. It confined 146 British prisoners, along with a few Dutch and Portuguese soldiers, after the nawab of Bengal, Sirajudaula, seized control of the city from the EIC. On 20 June 1756, 123 prisoners perished due to dehydration and suffocation in the cramped confines of Fort William. Robert Clive of the EIC found justification to invade Bengal and emerged victorious in the Battle of Plassey. However, it later emerged that the casualty figures had been highly exaggerated by survivors. Nevertheless, the tragedy deeply affected the European psyche.[19] Twain went on to assert that this memorial marked the laying of the foundation stone of the mighty British Empire. However, he was dismayed to find it in a dilapidated condition, just 140 years after its construction.

Twain was also informed about the vast jungles of India and the diverse wildlife that claimed thousands of human lives every year. In addition to labelling India as the Land of the Thug, the Land of the Plague, the Land of Famine, the Land of Giant Illusions and the Land of Stupendous Mountains, he also referred to it as the Land of Murderous Wild Creatures. He contrasted life in India with that of Paris, London and New York, where people succumbed to cancer, car accidents and suicides. In India, however, deaths often resulted from animal attacks. During those times, tigers claimed the lives of 5,000 Indians, leading the British government to retaliate by killing over 10,000 tigers. In total, the government exterminated a staggering 3,201,232 wild beasts during the six years of the 1890s. Wild animals paid a heavy toll for encroaching on villages that were once their domain. Snakes posed the greatest threat, causing 17,000 deaths per year, but around 110,000 of them were killed annually. The level of human atrocities appeared boundless.[20]

The First War of Independence, 1857

Twain felt a connection to the momentous event that had occurred almost forty years before his visit. He learned about the causes and effects of the great mutiny, now referred to as the First War of Independence.

In 1856, Lord Dalhousie of the East India Company annexed Oudh, citing internal mismanagement, in line with his Doctrine of Lapse, which stated that the British would take over a kingdom if there was misrule. The move sparked discontent among the sepoys of the Bengal Army, many of whom hailed from Oudh and could thus garner support within the province. A year later, in 1857, a full-fledged rebellion erupted in the state, and a siege was laid on the British Residency. The annexation of the kingdom of Oudh was later described by Sir Henry Lawrence as 'the most unrighteous act that was ever committed'[21].

On a particularly humid day in 1857, hundreds of mutineers assembled with hostile intent outside the plush Lucknow Residency, which housed 730 white soldiers and 500 women and children. Additionally, 480 loyal native soldiers acted as the first line of defence for the British. It was the British who trained natives to fight and kill fellow natives, and for a hundred years, it went smoothly. Native soldiers could readily subdue their own countrymen and were even willing to sacrifice their lives for a modest salary. The EIC never found such inexpensive and loyal employees elsewhere. This fact was widely known – the British ruled India with the assistance of native 'brown' people to minimize the risk to 'white' lives.

The siege persisted for three months, during which hundreds of white individuals were killed, and the remaining occupants began to suffer from starvation and disease. The Royal Residency transformed into a haunting, desolate place.[22]

The Relief of Lucknow, 1857, by Thomas Jones Barke.[23]

The wives of the British soldiers and officers, accustomed to every comfort in India, which was perhaps not even available back home, were forced to flee from the marauding native soldiers who, until recently, were subjected to every unreasonable whim of their masters. Twain was distressed to note that many British soldiers were killed with a sense of anger, as if their lives were as insignificant as insects. Many of the captured women prayed for a swift death, fearing the touch of the 'beastly brown natives' on their pristine white bodies.

Miss Wheeler defending herself against sepoys at Cawnpore in 1857. She has been portrayed as a defender of her 'Christian' honour over Hindus and Muslims.[24]

The British swiftly responded, outraged by such depraved actions by the natives. It was another matter that, for the past hundred years, they themselves had been inflicting atrocities on Indians. Sir Colin Campbell and his forces advanced from Cawnpore, capturing La-Martiniere College, Dilkusha, and other nearby locations one by one. Now, native British soldiers were engaged in combat against native ex-British soldiers, with the whites becoming collateral damage. Campbell's initial priority was to evacuate women and children, successfully rescuing 200 women and 250 children. Sir James Outram, summoned from Persia, harshly quelled the uprising upon his arrival.

In British annals, it is recorded that 2,392 British men, women and children died between 1857 and 1859 during what they perceived as the mutiny, while it's viewed as the First War of Independence from our perspective. In retaliation, approximately a million Indians lost their lives, including those who succumbed to famines and diseases that followed the carnage. The British were particularly incensed by reports of rapes of their women, as women's bodies were deemed to represent the community's honour, to be defended and avenged at any cost. Subsequent magisterial-level inquiries revealed that many of these reports were exaggerated or fictional, serving more to justify and prolong colonial rule than to reflect reality.[25]

Twain, however, conveniently chose to overlook these statistics. He lamented the fact that there were murmurs of discontent, yet the British failed to take notice. He expressed satisfaction with the ruthless manner in which they swiftly suppressed the mutiny and quelled so many natives. His primary concern, however, was why the mutiny occurred during peak summer, a time so uncomfortable for the aristocratic British. Overall, Twain only empathized with the British and their sufferings during the brief rebellion. He made no mention for the reasons for, or the wretched conditions of, the natives under English rule.[26]

Instead, he marvelled at the forts, mosques and tombs erected during the heyday of the Mohammedan emperors in Agra, Delhi and the surrounding areas. These structures were marvels of cost, magnitude and richness of materials and ornamentation, creations of grandeur that indeed made similar edifices elsewhere in the world seem tame and insignificant by comparison. During his visit to the Taj Mahal, he was astounded by its beauty. He went on to state that the Taj embodied humanity's highest potential in the creation of grace, beauty, exquisiteness and splendour. In his view, the Taj was where the work of a jeweller started after the architect had finished theirs. He was utterly enamoured with the monument:

> I mean to speak of only one of these many world renowned buildings, the Taj Mahal, the most celebrated construction in the earth, I had read a great deal too much about it. I saw it in the daytime, I saw it in the moonlight, I saw it near at hand, I saw it from a distance; and I knew all the time, that of its kind it was the wonder of the world, with no competitor now and no possible future competitor; and yet, it was not my Taj. My Taj had been built by excitable literary people.[27]

Hindu Customs

Like many European travellers of his time, Twain had clear preferences for people and things, placing Christians, Muslims, Buddhists and Hindus in that order. Throughout his book, there is a pervasive tone of revulsion towards Hindus and India. In the process, he exhibits continual racism, which, even by the standards of his era, is quite unacceptable. Naming his Hindu man Friday in India as Satan reflects his bias. It's doubtful that he would have dared to use such a name for a Christian or a Muslim character.

Twain also wrote extensively about Europeans' favourite topic – sati. He estimated that around 800 Hindu women would commit 'suicide' annually if the British allowed it. He was informed about a unique case of sati by Major William Sleeman, who was instrumental in abolishing sati as well as thugee, another scourge of India during that time. Sleeman had previously discovered a specimen of the dinosaur 'Titanosaurus Indicus' in Jabalpur in 1828, on the banks of the Narmada River. In honour of his contribution, the village where the dinosaur fossil was found was named Sleemanabad in Madhya Pradesh.

Sleeman, believing that widows were coerced into self-immolation, resulting in an extremely painful death, tried to dissuade a widow in 1828 from partaking in this gruesome practice. However, to his dismay, the woman remained resolute and sat near her husband's pyre stoically for four days without consuming any food or water. Eventually, Sleeman had to grant permission, but only after obtaining a written pledge from the family that they would never force any woman to commit sati in the future.[28]

Sleeman also noted six cases of feral children who had been raised by wolves in the jungles of the United Provinces and Central Provinces. He recounted these cases in his book, *Journey through the Kingdom of Oude in 1848–1850*. He verified that such a child was indeed rescued by Lieutenant John Moor after camping for a month in Seoni village, present-day Madhya Pradesh. In 1894, Rudyard Kipling, inspired by such intriguing accounts, created the famous character Mowgli in his renowned work, *The Jungle Book*.[29]

 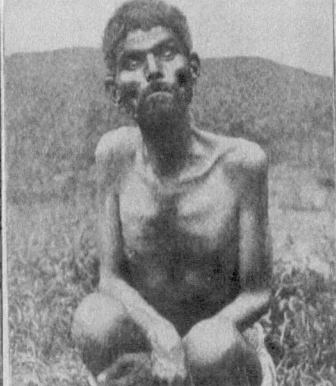

Sanichar, the 'Wolf Boy' of India.[30]

Thugee

Another favourite topic among travellers was thugee, and Twain delved into great detail describing this peculiar Indian practice. He started by portraying Kali as the goddess of thugs. Upon looking at her idol, he experienced instant revulsion, noting her red bloodshot eyes, garlands of skulls and protruding tongue. Witnessing animals like goats being sacrificed to her likely stirred his love for animals. However, despite this, he hunted numerous tigers during his brief stay in India and maintained a non-vegetarian diet every day of his life.

Twain quoted an 1839 government report authored by William Henry Sleeman:

> There is one very striking thing which I wish to call attention to. You have surmised from the listed callings followed by the victims of the Thugs that nobody could travel the Indian roads unprotected and live to get through; that the Thugs respected no quality, no vocation, no religion, nobody; that they killed every unarmed man that came in their way. [31]

Twain didn't hesitate to assert that all Indians possessed a criminal inclination, attributing the nonchalant roaming of thugs on highways to this alleged trait. He described thuggee or thuggery as an elaborate and long-drawn process, wherein thugs would befriend unsuspecting travellers over several days before ultimately robbing and murdering them. They employed a ceremonial handkerchief with a large metallic medallion to strangle their victim. Twain observed that thuggee was a hereditary profession, passed down from fathers to sons and even grandsons. Boys as young as sixteen and veterans as old as seventy were part of these deadly gangs. He noted that around 40,000 people were murdered annually in the early 1800s due to thuggery. Twain expressed surprise upon learning that thugs derived pleasure from their murderous acts. However, he conveniently overlooked the fact that white individuals also found pleasure in killing tigers, lions and even natives without just cause.[32]

THE THUGS WORSHIPPING KALEE.

Thugs worshiping Kali, around 1850.[33]

However, Twain neglected to mention one critical fact, which could have been deliberate – that most of these thugs, though not all, were Muslims. Despite maintaining their monotheistic faith, Muslim thugs appropriated Kali for thuggee, but they positioned her as a spirit subordinate to Allah. When Sleeman interrogated a Muslim thug, he revealed, 'In my heart, I take the name of God when I strangle a man, saying, "Allah, *tumhi* Malik!".'[34]

Twain experienced a rare moment of introspection at this juncture, where he acknowledged the violent history of Christianity as well. He exclaimed:

We white people are merely modified Thugs; Thugs fretting under
the restraints of a not very thick skin of civilization; Thugs who long
ago enjoyed the slaughter of the Roman arena, and later the burning
of doubtful Christians by authentic Christians in the public squares,
and who now, with the Thugs of Spain and Nimes, flock to enjoy the
blood and misery of the bull-ring. We have no tourists of either sex or
any religion who are able to resist the delights of the bull-ring when
opportunity offers; and we are gentle Thugs in the hunting season,
and love to chase a tame rabbit and kill it.[35]

The origin of thuggee remains shrouded in mystery, but Sleeman
attributed it to Indian rulers dismissing their armies when the
British occupied their kingdoms, thereby depriving many soldiers
of their livelihood and leaving them with no option but to resort
to thuggee. However, it's worth noting that thugs did operate
before the arrival of the British, albeit possibly on a smaller scale.[36]

A group of thugs strangling a traveller on a highway in India in the early 19th century.
Made for Capt. James Paton, assistant to the British Resident at Lucknow, 1829–40,
by an anonymous Indian artist.[37]

Almost all British officers regarded thuggee as an essential part of Hinduism, which they perceived as an evil and false sect rooted in idol worship. Sleeman played a significant role in associating Hinduism with this deadly activity, a connection that had not been made previously. However, it was this concept of religiously motivated murder that propelled thuggee to infamy worldwide. Popular works such as Philip Taylor's *Confessions of a Thug* and the cinematic blockbuster *Indiana Jones and the Temple of Doom* portrayed thuggee as primarily an evil religious cult. Many historians now believe that it served as a convenient tool for the British administration to depict thuggee, linked with Hinduism, as evidence of India's backwardness and to justify colonization.

Finally, under the administration of Governor-General William Bentick, the British government passed the Thuggee and Dacoity Suppression Act of 1836, criminalizing such activities and taking severe measures to suppress them.

However, similar forms of thuggee existed all over the world during that time; India was singled out for colonial purposes. Even in London, it manifested in a more brutal form in the early 18th century. However, the thugs there had a more polished name – highwayman. The outskirts of the city were the favoured haunt of highwaymen who would rob and kill the gentry travelling in their coaches from London to Windsor or Bath. Richard Turpin was the most infamous among them, but he was romanticized through numerous dramas and ballads. Highwaymen were known as road agents in the 19th-century American West, and as bushrangers in Australia.[38]

Caste System

Needless to say, Twain also found the caste system reprehensible and demeaning to humanity, viewing it as a major obstacle to India's national unity. Enraged by such a degrading system, he expressed strong condemnation, suggesting that a Hindu changing into an ass wouldn't lose anything unless you count his religion. He then advocated for conversion, believing it could help individuals rid themselves of the multitude of gods and godmen associated with Hinduism. In this regard, his scathing comments about the system are:

> It is a curious people. With them, all life seems to be sacred except human life. Even the life of vermin is sacred, and must not be taken. The good Jain wipes off a seat before using it, lest he cause the death of some valueless insect by sitting down on it. It grieves him to have to drink water, because the provisions in his stomach may not agree with the microbes. Yet India invented Thuggery and the Suttee. India is a hard country to understand. [39]

Twain wondered whether everything originated in India. Even trade unions and boycotts seemed to have roots in antiquity in India. He recounted a humorous anecdote about a sweeper class, despite being the lowest of the low castes, asserting their exclusive rights to clean the localities and going on strike. Since nobody else was willing to perform such a task, they had things their own way.

Epilogue

Twain ruefully observed that initially, India had a head start in the grand scheme of things. She established the first civilization, amassed material wealth ahead of others and was brimming with deep thinkers and astute intellects. With abundant mines, forests and fertile land, it seemed she should have maintained her lead and emerged as the world's dominant force, issuing laws and commands to every tribe and nation within it. However, there was never any potential for such dominance to materialize.

If there had only been one India and one language – of which there were eighty –fighting and quarrelling must have been the common business of life. With eighty nations and several hundred governments, unity of purpose and policy is impossible, and supremacy in the world cannot arise from such fragmented elements.[40]

Mark Twain donned multiple hats during his time in India, encompassing imperialist, Christian fanatic, racist, colonist and cultural chauvinist tendencies, with only fleeting sympathy for Hindus and India. Despite earning a considerable amount from his lecture tour of India, he did not retain many pleasant memories. He sums up his observations regarding India in the following words, albeit in his characteristic style of hyperbole:

> India has many names, and they are correctly descriptive. It is the Land of Contradictions, the Land of Subtlety and Superstition, the Land of Wealth and Poverty, the Land of Splendor and Desolation, the Land of Plague and Famine, the Land of the Thug and the Poisoner, and of the Meek and the Patient, the Land of the Suttee, the Land of the Unreinstatable Widow, the Land where All Life is Holy, the Land of Cremation, the Land where the Vulture is a Grave and a Monument, the Land of the Multitudinous Gods.[41]

8

Afanasy Nikitin

'Vast distances and the highest mountain ranges in the world separate the Soviet Union from India. But from old the peoples of the two great countries have lived in friendship, showing a keen interest in each other.'

—*Voyage beyond Three Seas*, Afanasy Nikitin

Afanasy Nikitin was a Russian merchant and explorer, renowned for his historic journey to India in the 15th century. Born in Tver, a town northeast of Moscow, Nikitin embarked on a remarkable expedition that yielded valuable insights into the trade routes, cultures and customs of the regions he traversed.

Afanasy Nikitin

Nikitin's journey to India occurred between 1470 and 1474. Setting out from Tver, he travelled southward, reaching the Persian Gulf. Continuing by sea, he eventually arrived in the port city of Chaul on the west coast of India. Nikitin spent several years in India, primarily exploring the regions of Gujarat and the Deccan.

One of the significant aspects of Nikitin's travels was his meticulous documentation of the Indian social, economic and cultural landscape. He also recorded his daily observations, thoughts and feelings, adding a personal touch to his scholarly work. He chronicled his observations in a detailed travelogue known as the *Khozhdeniye za tri morya* (Voyage beyond Three Seas or A Journey beyond the Three Seas). The text was uncovered in the archives of the Trinity St Sergius Monastery by Nikolai Karamzin, a prominent historian of 19th-century Russia.

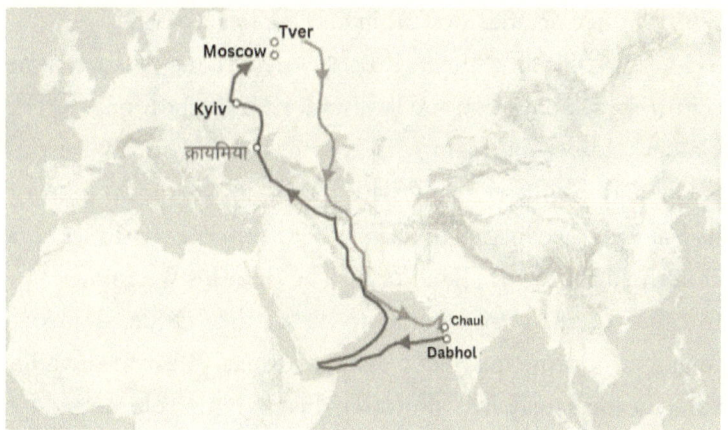

The journey of Nikitin.[1]

In this account, Nikitin provided descriptions of Indian society, its rulers, religious practices and the intricacies of trade. *Voyage beyond Three Seas* is considered one of the earliest firsthand accounts of India by a European traveller. Nikitin's adventurous journey captured the interest of both Russian and Western historians, as well as geopolitical thinkers interested in Russia's unique role in Asia. His detailed observations established him as an important figure in the history of early European exploration and interaction with India.

Notably, Nikitin's journey took place during the period when European maritime powers were beginning to explore sea routes to India. While his travels were not directly connected to these endeavours, his account provides valuable historical insights into the Indian subcontinent during that era. Nikitin holds the distinction of being the first Russian and the third European traveller to visit India, following in the footsteps of Italian travellers Marco Polo, who visited India in 1272, and Nicolo Conti, who journeyed to India in 1422 en route to Southeast Asia. The most prominent traveller of the millennium to India, Vasco da Gama, was still three decades away from his historical voyage.

During Nikitin's time, Russia was striving to overcome centuries of subjugation and devastation under the Mongols. The Golden Horde, the mammoth empire established by Genghis Khan and his descendant Batu Khan in the 13th century, had already declined. The Horde held Russian territories in a chokehold called the 'Tatar Yoke'. The Russians were now eager to expand their territory, and to do so, they needed someone to gather information about distant regions. Eager to serve his country and satisfy his own wanderlust, Nikitin volunteered for the job. One significant advantage he possessed was his knowledge of Persian, which was essential for travelling southward.

Nikitin's journey commenced as a business trip, with the initial leg leading him to the town of Niznij Novgorod. There, he joined Hasan-beg, the ambassador of the Shah of Sirvan (now Azerbaijan), who was returning from a diplomatic mission in

Moscow and embarking on a voyage down the Volga River. Passing through Kazan and Sarai, the river caravan, comprising ten Russians and several Muslim merchants, fell victim to an attack and plunder by Tatars (Turks) as they attempted to navigate past Astrakhan, a port city on the Caspian Sea. Nikitin lost his belongings but pressed on to Derbent, farther south along the Caspian Sea, with other survivors. The severity of the plunder prompted many to retreat, fearful of the perilous journey ahead. Nikitin noted in his book, *Voyage beyond Three Seas*, 'Whoever had something left in Rus returned to Rus; whoever had debts in Rus followed his nose.'

Finally reaching Persia after three weeks in 1466, Nikitin engaged in trading activities to earn some money. By that time, Persia was predominantly Islamic, with little to no presence of native Zoroastrians, who had either fled to India, converted or perished. Adhering to the adage, 'In Rome, do as Romans do', Nikitin assimilated into Muslim attire, customs and culture to integrate among the locals. Muslims were naturally pleased to see Europeans embracing their way of life. It is worth mentioning that both of these related religions often assert their belief that eventually, either all Christians will worship only Allah or all Muslims will embrace the Trinity.[2]

After spending approximately a year in Persia, Nikitin resolved to travel to India, a land reputedly flowing with milk and honey. His time in Persia failed to excite him as much as he had anticipated. Aware that Indian horses were not renowned for their quality, Nikitin purchased a horse to ride across India.

Historically, Indian kingdoms had imported sturdy oriental horses, but despite this, it remained challenging to acclimate them to the hot and humid climate of India. Many imported horses perished within a few years due to difficulties in adjusting to the Indian diet and weather conditions. This phenomenon was noted by Marco Polo in his travelogue, *The Travels of Marco Polo*.[3] Hindus did face a challenge when it came to their horses, as these animals were inferior in stamina, height and strength compared to their Central Asian and Arabic counterparts. The imported horses outclassed the Indian ones, providing their cavalry with the speed and flexibility to launch sudden attacks, overwhelm the enemy and retreat rapidly – a tactic that proved highly effective in battles.[4]

Setting out from the harbour of Hormuz in Persia, Nikitin, with his horse, sailed across the Arabian Sea to India, making several extended stops along the way. His first destination was the port of Cambay in present-day Gujarat, where he procured some indigo for future trade. After six weeks at sea, he eventually arrived at Chaul, now known as Revdanda, near Mumbai, much to the surprise of the locals, who had not encountered a white man in quite some time.

Chaul had been a renowned locale for centuries, as evidenced by inscriptions in the Kanheri caves near Mumbai expressing gratitude to jewellers from Chemulaka, its ancient name. In the following four decades, Revdanda would become a significant battleground as the Portuguese and Turks vied for supremacy in the Indian Ocean trade, culminating in a confrontation in 1508. Although the Portuguese were initially defeated, they would soon stake their claim on the entire western coast of India, with Surat remaining as their sole port of significance.

Nikitin recorded his first impression of India as follows:

[Everyone] goes naked; the women go bareheaded and with breasts uncovered, their hair plaited into braid. Many women are with child, and they bear children every year, and have many children. The men and women are all black. Wherever I went I was followed by many people who wondered at me, a white man.[5]

Nikitin's first interaction with people beyond Christians and Muslims left a negative impression on him. Consequently, he tried to live among Muslims exclusively. The region was under the Bahamani Sultanate, which derived revenue through frequent raids on the affluent neighbouring Hindu Vijayanagar kingdom. Muslims continually expanded their domains southward following the campaigns initiated by Allaudin Khilji and Mohammed Bin Tughlaq. However, being primarily invaders, they struggled to govern effectively and failed to establish enduring dynasties. Thus, it was not uncommon for slaves to overthrow and supplant the reigning sultan every few years.

The Hindu populace was vast, and Muslim rulers faced challenges in achieving mass conversion, unlike their counterparts in Arabia, Persia and Central Asia. Frustrated by this, they resorted to periodic large-scale Hindu genocides. They also appointed Muslims to key government positions, relegating Hindus to servitude. Muslims occupied the upper echelon of society, with a few Hindus having access to such ranks. Non-Muslims were prohibited from riding horses and subjected to burdensome jizya, a form of protection tax that was levied on non-Muslims. The sultans endeavoured to replicate the refined culture of Persia in India wherever possible. Nikitin also talked about the stark contrast in economic and social standing between the Muslim elite and the Hindu 'janta'. Muslims travelled in lavish gold palanquins with silver-mounted horse harnesses, accompanied by a retinue of elephants, horses, officials, servants and their harem. On the other hand, he described the Hindu warriors thus:

> The Hindoos walk all on foot and walk fast. They are all naked and bare-footed, and carry a shield in one hand and a sword in the other. Some of the servants are armed with straight bows and arrows.[6]

Note the usage of the word 'Hindoo' by Nikitin. Some leftist historians assert that the word 'Hindu' was coined as late as the 19th century.

After spending time in Persia, Nikitin became well-versed in Islamic traditions and language, feeling quite at home in India, but only in the company of Muslims. However, he often found himself in trouble due to his Christian background, despite Christians being considered 'people of the book' in Islam. This is a Muslim phrase referring to followers of cults that Muslims regard as having been guided by previous revelations and holy books. Christians and Jews are considered part of the book and can reside in Muslim lands by paying the hefty jizya tax. However, followers of religions like Hinduism and Buddhism are not considered worthy of living on earth.

Nikitin then adopted a Muslim name, Khoja Yusuf Khorassani, prompting many to speculate that he had converted to Islam in India. According to Islamic tenets, foreigners were entitled to trade without being citizens of the state for a year, after which they were required to either depart the country or embrace Islam. However, Nikitin had been in the Bahmani territory for only three months. Even then, his horse was seized by the wazir, Khan Asad.[7]

Asad informed Nikitin after he pleaded with a downcast expression:

'I will give you back your stallion and pay you a thousand pieces of gold, if only you will accept our Muslim faith. But if you should not adopt our Muslim faith, I shall keep the stallion and exact a ransom of a thousand pieces of gold from you.' And he gave me four days? Till Our Redeemer's Day, during the Fast of the Holy Mother of God. And the Lord had mercy upon me on His holy day, He kept not His mercy from me, miserable sinner, and left me not to perish at Junnar among the godless. Khoja Muhammad of Khorassan arrived on the eve of our Redeemer's Day, and I humbly begged him to plead for me. And he rode to the Khan in town, and persuaded him not to convert

me to his faith; he also took back my stallion. Such was the wonder
wrought by the Lord on Our Redeemer's Day. And so, my Christian
brothers of Rus', those of you who want to go to the land of India
must leave their faith in Rus' and invoke Muhammad before setting
out for the land of Hindustan.[8]

Khoja Muhammad, whom he had met in Russia during his
journey to Persia via the Volga, miraculously appeared in
Junnar that day and became his saviour. He helped Nikitin
in recovering his horse and also prevented him from undergoing
forced conversion. However, it illustrates the dire situation for
non-Muslims in Islamic India, where every day felt like a living
nightmare. Hindus often embraced Islam simply to escape the
harsh conditions. Throughout his book, Nikitin frequently wrote
phrases like, 'Such is the strength of the Muslim Sultan of India',
and the 'Muslim strength still holds good', highlighting the stark
contrast with the poverty and cultural disparity faced by Hindus.
He learned that the ancestry of most Muslim kings traced back
to Persia, especially from Khorasan, whereas 'moolniwasi'
(indigenous) Hindus were described a people who 'go on foot and
walk fast, and are all naked and barefoot'.[9]

In India, Nikitin always consistently dressed in Islamic
attire to assimilate. Scholar K.N. Chaudhuri, focussing on the
Indian Ocean region, observed that changing clothing signified
a conscious effort to alter his social identity. Nikitin further
observed that this process resembled conversion through
assimilation. By adopting a foreign culture over time, individuals
often converted voluntarily. This phenomenon mirrors historical
events, such as Christians in the Holy Land after the First Crusade
in 1099, coercing natives to adopt their practices, leading to
gradual conversions of entire native villages.

Such was the dominance of Muslims that the medieval sea
trade of India in the Red Sea and the Persian Gulf was entirely

controlled by Arabs, Persians, Jews and Armenians, while Hindus limited themselves to Southeast Asian trade.[10]

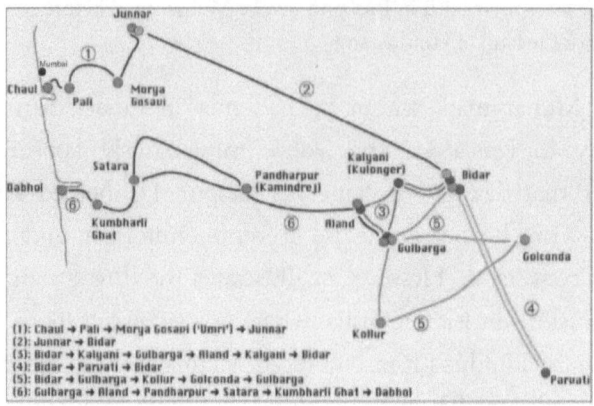

The Indian portion of Nikitin's journey and his stops in south India.[11]

During that time, the local chieftain served as a vassal to Bahmani Sultan Muhammad Shah III (1463–82). Since Sultan Muhammad Shah III ascended the throne as a child, Wazir Mahmud Gawan acted as his guardian. Intrigued by the reputed wealth of Bidar, Nikitin resolved to visit the city. After a journey via Junnar and Gulbarga, he arrived at Bidar (situated in present-day north Karnataka). Here, he sought to learn more about the Hindu population and eventually revealed his true identity as a Christian. Upon disclosing this, Nikitin found the doors of Hindu household opened to him, and he began socializing and dining with them. Through these interactions, he discovered that Hindus refrained from sharing meals with Muslims, whom they derisively called 'mleccha'.

He proceeded to elaborate on the distinctive dietary customs of Hindus in detail:

> The Hindoos eat no meat, no cow flesh, no mutton, no chicken. The banquets were all on pork; and pigs are in great abundance.

They take their meals twice a day, but not at night, and drink no wine nor mead; but with Mahommedans they neither eat nor drink. Their fare is poor. They eat not with one another nor with their wives, and live on Indian corn, carrots with oil, and different herbs. Always eating with the right hand, they will never set the left hand to anything nor use a knife; the spoon is unknown. In travelling everyone has a stone pot to cook his broth in. They take care that Mahommedans do not look into their pot, nor see their food, and should this happen they will not eat it; some, therefore, hide themselves under a linen cloth lest they should be seen when eating.... They sit down to eat, and wash their hands and feet, and rinse their mouths before they do so.[12]

In Bidar, he observed the sale of horses, silk and what he euphemistically referred to as 'black people' (indicating Hindus) in the market. Here, he sold his horses at favourable prices, reaping significant profits that he intended to utilize in his future travels. Gawan, himself a foreigner hailing from Persia, was impressed by Nikitin and showed favouritism towards him. Nikitin reciprocated this favour, as evident from his description of the opulence of Gawan's palace in Bidar. He wrote:

> The Sultan's palace has seven gates, with a hundred guards and a hundred kaffir scribes at each gate; some of them register those coming in and others, those going out; but strangers are barred from the palace. And the palace is very beautiful, with fretwork and gilt all over it, and its every stone is fretted and very beautifully painted in gold, and inside the palace, there are sundry vessels.[13]

He travelled to Parvattum, a sacred place for Hindus, and to the Mallikarjuna Jyotirlinga at Srisailam in Andhra Pradesh, akin to Jerusalem or Mecca. He observed their prayers to the idols and their reverence for the cow as their mother, which distinctly made him uncomfortable. He, however, was awestruck by the size of the temple complex and stated that it must be half the size of his hometown, Tver. Thousands of pilgrims arrived, travelling on foot, in oxen carts and even on elephants. He further noted that the temple sustained the economy of the entire region.

Like every other foreigner, the caste system intrigued him, and he observed that people of different castes neither intermarried nor dined together, resulting in social fragmentation. He noted the existence of eighty-four castes at the time, implying significant differences among them, to the extent that he referred to them as 'faiths'. He also observed the minimal clothing worn by Hindus and their numerous dietary restrictions. This marked his brief and only interaction with Hindus during his four-year stay in India. He proceeded to write about Hindus, 'The people [Indians] are all black and wicked, and the women are shameless; everywhere there is witchcraft, robbery, lying, and potions with which they kill their masters.'[14] He also discussed the Indian fascination with fair skin, especially among Hindu women, as fairer children were often associated with upper castes. He insinuated that Indian women often expressed a desire to engage in physical relations with him in hopes of bearing fair-skinned children.

He believed that the concept of one God contributed to the political, financial and military superiority of monotheistic religions over polytheistic Hinduism. He found Hinduism objectionable, primarily because he considered the idols unattractive:

> [The But] wears no clothing, save that his buttocks are wrapped in a cloth; his face is that of an ape. And the other buts are stark naked, they wear nothing, and their buttocks are uncovered; and Buts wives are carved naked, in all their shame, and with children.[15]

Regarding their dietary preferences, Nikitin observed that Hindus consumed mutton, fowl, eggs and pork but never beef. Their staple diets included rice, khichdi, vegetables, glee, milk and wine made from coconuts. Cow dung served as fuel for cooking meals, and its ashes were used for painting their faces, foreheads and even their bodies.

Nikitin's primary task was to gather information about India for prospective Russian travellers and merchants, so a significant portion of his book focussed on commerce. In this context, he wrote about Calicut:

> A big harbor on the Indian Sea, and God forbid that any ship should pass by it; no one who sails past it will cross the sea unscathed. And it produces pepper, ginger, nutmeg, cinnamon, cloves, spices, adrak [a type of ginger], and many kinds of herbs. And everything is cheap there; and slaves are very good; they are black.[16]

When informed about the diamond mines in Golconda, he instantly became interested and visited them at the next available opportunity. However, unlike Tavernier, he did not engage in diamond trading. Two centuries later, Tavernier would amass wealth from these same mines.

Though he never journeyed to Ceylon, he recounted a myth about Adam, wherein atop a high mountain lay the imprint of a human foot, purportedly belonging to Father Adam during his time there. According to the legend, Adam, the first human, spent several years in the vicinity following his expulsion from the Garden of Eden. However, Buddhism, one of the oldest religions, had already laid claim to it, asserting that the footprint belonged to Buddha when he visited the area to deliver a sermon. Furthermore, Hinduism, the most ancient religion, claims that it belongs to Ravana.

After spending almost four years in India, he grew homesick and resolved to return. He sailed from Dabhol (in the Ratnagiri district of Maharashtra) to Ethiopia, then to Muscat and from there to Russia. His return journey was not without incident. The ship was thrown off course by a storm but managed to reach the shore safely. Following this, he spent some time there before continuing his journey, travelling through Persia and then to the Black Sea coast of

Turkey. The title of his book, *Journey beyond Three Seas*, reflects his travels across the Caspian, Arabian and Black Seas.

In the Turkish port of Trabzon, he encountered trouble when he was arrested and his belongings confiscated on suspicion of being a spy. Fortunately, his captors showed no interest in his notes, and he was able to persuade them to release him. He then crossed the Black Sea to Feodosia, where Russian merchants generously lent him money to settle his debts and facilitate his return home. However, his health deteriorated significantly due to the hardships of his arduous journey. In 1475, Nikitin passed away near Smolensk, before reaching home, at the age of forty.

Nikitin offered the following advice to fellow Russian traders, 'And so, my Christian brothers of Rus', those of you who want to go to the land of India must leave their faith in Rus' and invoke Muhammed before setting out to the land of Hindustan.'[17]

In 1957, a Hindi-Russian film titled *Pardesi*, jointly directed by Khwaja Ahmad Abbas and Vasili Pronin, was produced, featuring Nargis in the lead role. However, the film conveniently omitted any depiction of Nikitin's anti-Hindu or anti-Indian sentiments. On the contrary, it depicted him staying in Hindu households and developing feelings for a Hindu girl, a scenario unlikely to occur in reality even in Nikitin's dreams.

Despite being deeply impressed by Muslims, his return was marked by disappointment, as evident from the following statement, 'Those Mussulman dogs have lied to me, saying I should find here plenty of our goods; but there is nothing for our country. All goods for the land of Mussulmans, as pepper and colours, and these are cheap.'[18]

Even though his account can be undoubtedly deemed as anti-Hindu, even by the standards of that era, it provides thoroughly interesting data, often eccentric, about his journey and about 15th-century south India.

Poster of the film *Pardesi*.[19]

The Monument of Afanasy Nikitin in Feodosia, Crimea.[20]

In 1955, a memorial was erected in Russia in his honour. An interesting backstory exists, wherein Nehru, during Soviet President Nikita Khrushchev's visit to India, inquired if there was a statue of Nikitin in Russia. Khrushchev, unaware of the existence of such a statue, nevertheless replied in the affirmative. With Nehru's return visit imminent, Khrushchev, prompted by a call from Delhi, ordered the construction of a statue of Nikitin be built without delay.

A special cover was released in New Delhi on 11 October 2021 to celebrate the 550th Anniversary of Afanasy Nikitin's visit to India.[21]

Nikitin introduced India to the Russian populace through his vivid portrayal of its diverse customs and ways of life. Despite not being a philosopher or intellectual, his book displays a keen sense of observation. His narrative generated a profound romantic fascination with India in Russia, leading to the development of a rich tradition of Indology. This laid the foundation for an enduring friendship between the governments of Russia and India.

9

Fanny Parkes and Other British Women Explorers

'She (India) has left indelible imprints on one fourth of the human race in the course of a long succession of centuries. She has the right to reclaim ... her place amongst the great nations summarizing and symbolizing the spirit of humanity. From Persia to the Chinese sea, from the icy regions of Siberia to Islands of Java and Borneo, India has propagated her beliefs, her tales, and her civilization.'

—Sylvia Levi (French scholar)

During the British colonial era, numerous adventurous women challenged societal norms by embarking on explorations to various parts of the world, including India. Their travels were frequently documented through journals, letters and books, providing invaluable insights into the cultures and landscapes they encountered.

These intrepid women explorers defied societal expectations, embarking on extensive journeys and leaving behind invaluable accounts of their experiences in India. Through their writings, they enriched our understanding of the cultural, social and political complexities of British India during the colonial era.

While many of these women were merely pawns of the empire, a small minority embraced the local culture and actively engaged in the Indian freedom struggle.

British Women in India

In the early 1700s, India remained under Muslims rule, and it was perceived as unsafe territory for British women. The EIC was hesitant to cover the expenses of female family members accompanying their officers, as they were keenly aware that many would struggle to endure the hot and humid tropical climate of India. The prevalence of mosquitoes and flies further compounded the challenges, leading to widespread illness and mortality among those who ventured to the region.

In its infancy, the British Raj was unquestionably a male-dominated sphere. Men held exclusive control over the army, police and bureaucracy. Due to restrictions, only a few officers were permitted to bring their wives, resulting in a mere 200 white women residing in India among thousands of British men in the early 18th century. Even in rapidly growing cities like Bombay, the presence of British women was scarce, with only sixteen recorded during that period.

The majority of British women in India were family members, with a few additional maids, governesses and teachers. Some also arrived as part of missionary groups, aiming to civilize and convert the 'brown people', as women were considered to be more efficient agents for conversion. They sought to Westernize Hindu women, although not Muslims, encouraging them to adopt the mannerisms, attire, cuisine, eating habits, housekeeping and demeanour of Victorian ladies. Organizations such as the Red Cross, Young Women's Christian Association and Girl Guides were prominent missionary agents at the time, facilitating conversions to lead the 'beastly' natives to the 'one and only true God'. Despite the missionary agenda, these organizations also engaged in health, educational and other charitable activities.

With regards to permitting women to enter the colonies, the British adhered to the dictum of the Roman historian Cornelius Tacitus:

> The rule which forbade women to be taken to provinces or foreign countries was salutary. A female entourage stimulates extravagance in peacetime and timidity in war.... Women are not only frail and easily tired. Relax control, and they become ferocious, ambitious schemers, circulating among the soldiers, ordering company-commanders about.... The wives attract every rascal in a province.[1]

By this time, the British were beginning to recreate England in India, akin to how the Mughals and Delhi sultans had replicated the lavish lifestyle of Persia in pre-British era. With a bevy of Indian servants at their disposal, the comfort of their lives in palatial mansions located in cantonments on the outskirts of every Indian city far exceeded that of their homes back in England.

Only after the Battle of Plassey in 1757, when the British had firmly established themselves, did India become an inviting destination for British women. Following this pivotal battle, British men enjoyed unfettered power, unlimited money, expansive palatial residences, abundant hunting opportunities and an endless supply of native male and female servants. While male servants ran errands and did sundry jobs, indigenous women were expected to perform household chores and fulfil their masters' desires. The EIC actively discouraged marriages with Indian women to maintain colonial superiority and racial purity throughout their rule. Going native was considered the gravest transgression. Despite their lavish lifestyles, British men yearned for the emotional support of their own women.

In the absence of European women, British officers maintained Indian mistresses during their tenure in India, regardless of the fate of those hapless women afterward. Many of these relationships resulted in illegitimate children. For instance, Job Charnock, the founder of Calcutta, fathered three children with his Hindu mistress, whom he had saved from a sati funeral pyre. Similarly, in the 1790s, George Dick, the governor of Bombay, housed a Maratha woman in his residence. However, the woman faced accusations of tyranny, corruption and even espionage on behalf of Maratha pirates.

Sir David Ochterlony, who served as the resident of Delhi from 1803 to 1825, reportedly had no less than thirteen Indian mistresses. Even individuals of high esteem, such as Lord Teignmouth, who served as governor-general (1793–98) and founded the British and Foreign Bible Society, maintained such relationships. Additionally, Col James Skinner (1778–1841), the creator of the elite regiment 'Skinner's Horse', was rumoured to have had fourteen wives and fathered eighty children.[2] Nearly all white men deemed Indian wives or mistresses more suitable compared to British women, who were viewed as 'demanding'. Samuel Sneade Brown, a magistrate in the Indian Civil Service in the 1830s, remarked:

> I have observed that those who have lived with a native woman for any length of time never marry a European... so amusingly playful, so anxious to oblige and please, that a person after being accustomed to their society shrinks from the idea of encountering the whims or yielding to the fancies of an Englishwoman.[3]

The empire rested on three pillars – Christianity, commerce and copulation. Company officials were aware of the carnal needs of its soldiers. Although the practice of living with Indian women was never officially condoned by the company, it refrained from punishing those who engaged in such relationships, leading to a peculiar dilemma. The company feared unrest if the number of Indian mistresses reached a critical mass. Excessive visits to brothels posed health risks to soldiers, who were considered costly imports. While preventing such visits could result in unnatural relationships among soldiers, the British opted for the next best solution – establishing brothels within the seventy-five cantonments. Indian women were housed there after undergoing check-ups, and sexual interaction with non-whites was typically prohibited thereafter. In Lucknow, for instance, the brothel was a huge mansion with fifty-five rooms. On average, each cantonment area accommodated 3,750 white soldiers, with approximately 100 Indian women employed to serve them. The prostitutes were paid well, ensuring the sustainability of the system.[4]

However, criticism against the system continued to mount over time. The company found itself at a loss regarding how to address these concerns until two separate incidents provided a resolution.

Changing Geopolitical Scenario

After the opening of the Suez Canal in 1869, which significantly shortened the voyage from London to Bombay from six months to just three weeks, a wave of white women started arriving in India. This influx coincided with the First War of Independence in 1857, prompting the British government to implement even stricter segregation between the ruling class and the 'slaves'. Consequently, norms regarding travel for British women were considerably relaxed. Among these women was a special group known as the 'Fishing Fleets' or 'Cargo of Young Damsels'. This period marked the height of colonialism, with many eligible men stationed abroad, resulting in a surplus of unmarried women in Britain. In search of suitable grooms, these women travelled to colonies like India. Initially staying with friends and families, they began their search for partners immediately upon arrival. The success rate was high, as many men also sought European feminine companionship amidst the challenges of life in India. Those who were unsuccessful in finding a match were mockingly referred to as 'Returned Empties'. As far as Indians were concerned, all white women were collectively referred to as 'memsahibs'. The term 'mem' originated from 'ma'am', while 'sahib' was a Persian term of respect for people of higher status.

In his travel journal, J.R. Ackerley, a close friend of E.M. Forster, recounts an anecdote shared by an Englishwoman living in India. The memsahib was returning to her bungalow in the evening, accompanied by a servant, when a krait – one of India's most venomous snakes – slithered onto the path. Ackerley quotes the memsahib as saying, 'Then the servant did a thing absolutely without precedent in India – he touched me! – he put his hand on my shoulder and pulled me back. Of course, if he hadn't done that, I should undoubtedly have been killed; but I didn't like it all the same, and got rid of him soon after.'

This anecdote can be interpreted as representative of the empire, with the key elements of a hostile environment and confused natives. The Englishwoman in India is at the centre, either unwittingly or deliberately blind to the native's loyalty, depending on one's point of view. The unspoken fear is that native men will lust after white women. Above all, the story perpetuates the stereotype of the memsahibs. They were frequently blamed for increasing inter-racial distrust and hostility. Memsahibs were portrayed as intolerant, viciously racist and abusive of servants, with interests limited to gossip and extramarital affairs. Not surprisingly, this image of the memsahib has remained consistent even today.[5]

British society was highly class-conscious, with its hierarchies surpassing even caste distinctions. A women's social status was largely determined by her husband's rank, and they were acutely aware of these divisions. The woman married to a husband with the highest official station was called the 'burra memsahib', and she held considerable influence in the women's world. She was given priority seating in venues, such as theatres, trains and ships. She also enjoyed the finest food and wine. The wives of lower-ranking officers and soldiers always deferred to her. Native women were typically assigned the most menial tasks in European households. In a nutshell, the burra memsahib was always the first choice and had the last word. While they engaged in charitable work on the sidelines, they also facilitated conversions among the native population. This tradition of 'ladies' club' continues in India within various governmental offices, armed forces and even PSUs (public sector undertakings).

British women enjoyed a privileged life in India. Miss Emily Bayley, an English memoirist, once embarked on a tour of north and east India by boat on the Ganges and remarked that 'it was one continual picnic from morning until night'. On trains, too, British women had separate ladies' compartments, allowing them to observe Indian life closely from the safety of these chambers. Their relationship with the natives was often characterized by an 'Us vs Them' mentality or, at worst, a master–slave dynamic. The latter represented a cruel and brutal world, marked by horrible rapes, merciless beatings, daylight murders and savage torture.

The arrival of European women in India hastened the decline of Indian mistresses in colonial bedrooms:

> As wives they hastened the disappearance of the Indian mistress. As hostesses they fostered the development of exclusive social groups in every civil station. As women they were thought by Englishmen to be in need of protection from lascivious Indians.[6]

During the 1910s, especially after the conclusion of the First World War, an increasing number of nationalist white women started travelling to India, displaying sympathy towards India's demand for independence. Britain's declining interest in India, as its best officers were preoccupied with European conflicts during the world wars, further facilitated this trend. Notable figures such as Annie Besant, Freida Bedi and Margret Noble (Sister Nivedita) were among these women. However, Noble and Bedi stood out they fully embraced the 'native' culture and lifestyle.

Noble made a truthful observation about the 'shakti' wielded by Hindu women, emphasizing the need for proper channelization:

> Woman alone represented that unbroken continuity with a precolonial past through her residence in that uncolonized space, the zenana. Through her very domesticity, extended now beyond the 'stones' and 'walls' of her home to include 'land and people', the Indian woman was a repository of resistance.[7]

A British family with an Indian maid.[8]

Among these travelling women, only a select few possessed the intellectual acumen to critically observe and document the events in India. The remainder appeared distant, bored and irritated. As Wilfrid Scawen Blunt, a rare British anti-imperialist in the 1880s, remarked, 'These memsahibs were responsible for half the bitter feelings between the races.'[9]

The remaining women were content with leisure activities like playing bridge and rummy. Behind their husbands' backs, they openly flirted with younger, handsome British men. The stereotype of the memsahib is one of melancholy and frailty, barely tolerant, vindictive towards the locals, abusive towards their servants, usually bored, viciously gossiping, prone to extramarital affairs, displaying cruel insensitivity towards Indian women and hopelessly isolated from them.[10]

To shield them from the Indian heat and humidity, hill stations were developed across India, offering them a semblance of England within India itself. As author Amy Baker wrote in 1931, 'Up in the hills young men are rare; down in the plains young women are rare. Young men are spoiled in the hills and lost in the plains.'[11]

British Women's Perception of India

Most intellectual women arrived in India after 1857, and a time when the British perception of Indian culture had undergone a complete metamorphosis. In the late 1700s, figures like William Jones were fascinated by India and established institutions like the Asiatic Society, which played a role in deciphering the Brahmi script. During this period, sites such as Ajanta, Sanchi and Amravati were also unearthed. The Vedas and Upanishads were extensively translated into English, albeit incorrectly. In the eyes of Britishers, India was viewed as 'this wonderful country'. However, the events of 1857 marked a turning point, altering this perception entirely. India was suddenly portrayed as dirty and beastly. The gap between the races, which had already been significant, now widened even further.

However, efforts to depict India in a negative light were already underway. James Mill's *History of India* (1817) and the *East India Register* (1818), later known as the *Civil List*, provided unfavourable assessments of the Indian people. These perspectives influenced British opinions and writings about India.

Unfortunately, the female perspective did not differ significantly from the male viewpoint, as both remained focused on issues such as sati, thuggee and the caste system. Similar to European males, they harboured a favourable disposition towards Muslims, while Hindus were invariably labelled as heathens and idolaters. Most of them advocated for British colonial policies aimed at implementing social reforms among Hindus. However, strangely, they remained silent on matters concerning Muslims.

Only in matters concerning the zenana, the part of the house reserved for the women of the household, could British women offer genuine insights. They often reported on the miserable lives of women in these quarters. Similar to other schisms created by the British among Indians, they portrayed Indian men as oppressors and women as oppressed. The underlying message, to quote the famous words of Indian scholar Gayatri Spivak, was 'white men saving brown women from brown men'. Female travellers willingly served as pawns in justifying the rationale for the empire to redeem 'fallen natives', to carry the 'white man's burden', to seize the chance to 'do good' and to ease some guilt associated with inflicting unbridled violence. In this way, the writings of female travellers mirrored British colonial policies.[12]

However, resistance to the imposing British social reforms persisted among Hindu women, as with other aspects of colonial rule. Contrary to popular perception, it was often the women who held sway over men within the household. As noted by social reformer Mary Carpenter, 'It is everywhere felt among the enlightened that the stronghold of idolatry, and all its attendant evils, is in the home.'[13]

Many of the female travellers concluded that it was the Indian women who needed to be addressed if the British hoped to culturally subjugate India. Reflecting on the resistance to

British dominance, British-era author, Maud Diver, remarked, 'It was not the man, that reputed tyrant, who most effectually barred the way to progress, it is the gentle, invisible, woman whose reserve of obstinacy, all the wild horses in the Empire would fail to move.'[14]

Another author, Barbara Wingfield-Stratford, echoed similar sentiments in 1922, 'The Indian woman, more than the men of the country, voluntarily follow an unpractical, uncomfortable, and unworldly wise course of literal obedience to some idealistic concept.'[15] Norah Rowan Hamilton, an author, similarly resonated, 'This was the unreasonable, illogical space that resisted colonization and, thus, civilization; it is therefore within the zenana that women must first be freed.'[16]

Even the Simon Commission in 1930 acknowledged the significant influence wielded by Hindu women throughout society in India:

> No one with any knowledge of India would be disposed to underrate the power its women wield within the confines of the household. The danger is that, unless the influence is illumined with knowledge ...its weight may be cast against the forces of progress.[17]

Credit must be attributed to white, thoughtful women for correctly identifying the power source of Hindu society, as women have been revered as Shakti since time immemorial. Annie Besant, a true Indophile and leader of the Home Rule movement in the 1920s, harnessed the reservoirs of 'heroism, endurance, and self-sacrifice of the feminine nature' within the movement. She hoped, 'In the representatives of Shakti will be the certain triumph of India in the nation and the Indian home.'[18] For this precise purpose, India was depicted as Bharat Mata, with the first sketch created by Abanindranath Tagore in 1905.

'Bharat Mata', a painting by Abanindranath Tagore.[19]

Margaret Cousins, a theosophist, earnestly pleaded that 'Indian women express the needs of the mother-half of humanity', as the present world order needed 'the creative and conserving qualities of women'.

In hindsight, Katie Hickman, author of *She-Merchants, Buccaneers & Gentlewomen*, succinctly captures the situation: 'If it were not for the snobbery and racial prejudice of the memsahibs there would, somehow, have been far greater harmony and accord between the races.'[20]

Prominent Women Travellers

During these two centuries, several European women travelled to India throughout the British colonial era, documenting their experiences, observations and encounters with the diverse Indian culture and society. Despite their often-biased perspectives, they significantly contributed to the understanding of India.

Following are the notable European women travellers to India during that period:

Frances Steele

Frances was the first European woman to reach India, defying the company's explicit prohibition on women travelling to India, despite numerous pleas from its factors and sailors who wished to have their wives accompany them. Pregnant and madly in love with her husband Richard, Frances was determined not to leave his side, even for a minute, and was prepared to go to any lengths to remain with him.

As mentioned earlier, Mariam was travelling to England with her husband, William Hawkins, from India on a ship. Tragically, William passed away during the voyage. Mariam subsequently fell in love with another EIC employee, Captain Gabriel Towerson, during this journey. They later married, and after spending two years in London, they decided to return to India in 1617. It was in London that Mariam met Frances, who cleverly disguised herself as Mariam's maid. Despite Frances managing to reach India, Thomas Roe, the next official to India, discovered the escapade. While Roe was infuriated upon learning of the situation, he found himself unable to take action due to the delicate situation involved. Collectively, these women led Roe and the company to view all English wives in India as 'encumbrances'. However, she remained an inspiration for all European women in the coming years.

Jane Smart

Jane Smart, who lived in Madras during the early 1700s, stands as one of the pioneering female European travellers of her time. Her letters to her son, penned in 1743, span just eight pages. In these letters, she recounts the visit of the nawab of Arcot to the British governor in Madras. While the literary quality of the letters may be deemed modest, they hold significant historical importance. These letters are preserved in Henry Davison Love's work *Vestiges of Old Madras* (volume II).

Jemima Kindersley

Her husband, Colonel Nathaniel Kindersley of the Bengal Artillery, had previously travelled to India. Inspired by his travels, she embarked on her own voyage to India in June 1764. Arriving in Pondicherry in June 1765, her journey included stops in Tenerife, Brazil and South Africa. Her stay in India lasted until 1769. Kindersley meticulously chronicled her extensive voyage, spanning sixty-eight letters. These letters, detailing her experience during her five-month-long stay at the Cape of Good Hope and the East Indies, were published in 1777 under the title *Letters from the Island of Teneriffe, Brazil, the Cape of Good Hope and the East Indies by Mrs. Kindersley.*

Biddy Timms

Perhaps the only one to have fully embraced the 'native' culture, Timms went so far as to marry an Indian Shia Muslim during that era. She met Meer Hassan Ali in London, where he worked as a teacher. They fell in love, got married and relocated to Lucknow in 1817. To navigate the conservative Muslim society, she diligently acquired a working knowledge of Hindi. However, she struggled to reconcile with the strict customs of Islam and her husband's decision to take multiple wives. After a few years, she returned to London but still wrote a sympathetic account of Muslims titled *Observations on the Mussulmauns of India*, which was published in two volumes in 1832.

Emily Eden

Emily Eden, sister of the first Earl of Auckland, George Eden, visited India in the 1830s. Her collection of letters titled *Up the Country: Letters Written to Her Sister from the Upper Provinces of India* (1866) documents her adventures. Through her writings, readers gain invaluable insights into the social life and customs prevalent in India during that era.

Isabella Bird

In the late 1800s, Isabella Bird, a Scottish traveller and writer, visited India. Her travelogue *Among the Tibetans* (1894), chronicles her journey through the Himalayas, exploring regions such as Ladakh and Kashmir. During her time in India, the maharaja of Kashmir generously granted her a plot of land to construct a hospital, which she named the John Bishop Memorial Hospital, equipped with sixty beds and a women's dispensary. Additionally, in 1891, she travelled from Baluchistan to Persia and Armenia to study the source of the Karun River.

Sophia Dobson Collet

In the 1870s, Sophia Dobson Collet, a British social reformer, travelled to India. Her autobiography, *Miss Collet of the Department of Agriculture: An Autobiography* (1884), provides a comprehensive account of her travels, documenting her experiences and observations during her time in India.

Josephine Butler

Her case was unique as she never physically travelled to India, yet her impact on Indian women was profound. A prominent 19th-century British social reformer, Butler dedicated her life to improving the rights and welfare of women, particularly those facing marginalization and oppression. Her advocacy extended beyond Britain to India, where she advocated for women's right and challenged the injustices perpetuated by the British colonial administration.

Her efforts in prostitution reform earned her national and international recognition. In the mid-19th century, prostitution was rampant in Britain, with many women, including girls as young as twelve, being forced into the profession due to poverty and lack of options. Shocked by the harsh treatment these women endured, Butler became a vocal champion of their rights. She actively campaigned for the repeal of the Contagious Diseases Acts, which authorized the forcible examination and treatment of women suspected of prostitution, a practice derogatorily termed 'surgical' or 'steel rape'. Her efforts were instrumental in the repeal of these laws in 1886.

Josephine Butler's work in Britain soon extended to India, where she became aware of the plight of women who were victims of the British colonial administration. Although the UK had repealed the Contagious Diseases Acts, similar laws were still in effect during the British Raj in India, subjecting Indian women working for soldiers in British cantonments to cruel forced examinations. Through her efforts, in 1888, the controversial law was repealed; however, the British government soon enacted a similar but toned-down law.

Like others of her era, she never condemned British imperialism and even went on to remark, 'With all her faults, looked at from God's point of view, England is the best, and the *least* guilty of the nations.'[21]

Annie Besant

Annie Besant, an Englishwoman and social activist, relocated to India in the late 1800s and played an important role in India's independence struggle. While she was not a conventional travel writer, her speeches, articles and books provide insights into her experiences and perspectives on Indian society. The noted philosopher Jaddu Krishnamurthy was her adopted son.

The stamp featuring Sister Nivedita.[22]

Margaret Noble

She was an Irish teacher, author and social activist who later became a disciple of Swami Vivekananda. During her teenage years, she became disillusioned with Christianity and was seeking an alternative religion when she happened to meet Swami Vivekananda. Her life changed completely at that point, and she embraced Sanatan Dharma as the true Dharma.

Regarding her journey to Sanatan, she once remarked in a lecture in Bombay in 1902: 'I plunged into the study of the religion of Buddha, and became more and more convinced that the salvation he preached was decidedly more consistent with the Truth than the preachings of the Christian religion.'[23]

She arrived in Calcutta in 1898 and established a girls' school there. Just a year later, in 1899, a plague swept through Calcutta, claiming the lives of lakhs of people. She tended to the sick and managed to save many from brink of death.

Swami ji bestowed upon her the beautiful Sanskritic name Nivedita, and thereafter, she became associated with the Ramakrishna Mission. Flourishing as a writer, she delivered lectures across India, specializing in Indian religions and culture. She urged India's youth to work selflessly, aligning with Swami Vivekananda's ideals, for the betterment of their nation. She exhorted Indian artists like Abanindranath Tagore, Nandlal Bose, Ananda Coomaraswamy and even E.B. Havell to cultivate an Indian school of art rooted in ancient heritage.

She authored the book *Cradle Tales of Hinduism* in 1907, which compiled stories from the Ramayana, Mahabharata and Puranas.

Marjorie Sykes

A British educator and writer named Marjorie Sykes visited India and became involved in the Indian independence movement. Her book *No Place for Ladies: The Untold Story of Women in the Crimean War* (1959) includes details about her experiences in India.

'The Life of a Memsahib', unknown photographer, Mussoorie, 1875.[24]

Freda Bedi

Born Freda Marie Houlston, she pursued a major in philosophy and fell in love with Baba Pyare Lal 'BPL' Bedi, a Sikh from Lahore, eventually marrying him despite family opposition. Even in Europe, she gracefully adorned herself in sarees and became a notable figure in London. She authored and edited four books about India's freedom struggle.

Freda, along with her husband, arrived in India in 1934 and taught English at a women's college in Lahore. She was already a nationalist and regularly contributed articles to the *Tribune*. She was even imprisoned by the British during the Second World War, probably the only instance where the British jailed a British woman in India. In 1948, Freda even enlisted in a women's militia to defend Srinagar from invading Pakistani terrorists, especially the Afridi tribals. Following Independence, she acquired Indian citizenship, underwent a Vipassana course and embraced Buddhism, eventually becoming a Buddhist nun.

Freda Bedi and Baba Pyare Lal Bedi at Nishat Bagh, Srinagar, 1948.[25]

In 1959, when the Dalai Lama fled to India to escape Chinese tyranny, she guided him to the Buddhist shrines in Delhi. She also founded the Young Lamas Home School in Dalhousie, Himachal Pradesh, where she trained young Tibetans in Buddhist teachings. Through this endeavour, she translated numerous Buddhist texts into English and introduced Tibetan Buddhism to the Western world. The renowned Hindi film actor Kabir Bedi is her son.

Fanny Parkes

Fanny Parkes was arguably one of the most vibrant female travellers of her time, and her story deserves thorough exploration.

Krishna with his gopis, painted by Fanny Parkes.[26]

Living with her husband in Calcutta and Allahabad from 1822 to 1846, she developed a deep affection for Indian culture and heritage. Mastering Hindustani, she effortlessly engaged in conversations with the locals. Displaying her independent mindset and offering fresh insights into Hindu customs, she extensively documented the disparity between the indulgent lifestyles of the British and the famine-stricken, starving natives. Yet, she often succumbed to the stereotyped European narratives of sati, thuggee and caste, vehemently denouncing them. Throughout, she showed a partiality towards Muslims and allocated minimal attention to Hindus in her writings. Her memoirs were published under the title *Wanderings of a Pilgrim in Search of the Picturesque during Four and Twenty Years in the East with Revelations of Life in the Zenana.*

Once, the British government entertained the idea of selling the Taj Mahal to the highest bidder. On 26 July 1831, under William Bentick, the first governor-general of India, the British government published a tender in the Calcutta-based British newspaper *John Bull* (later *The Statesman*) for its dismantling. Seth Laxmichand Jain, a Mathura-based trader and a banker to several maharajas, emerged as the highest bidder, offering Rs 2 lakh. Referred to as the 'Rothschild of India' by the London-based newspaper, *The Times*, Seth's bid was deemed too low and was consequently rejected. However, when the bid was reopened a few months later, Seth offered a substantially higher amount of Rs 7 lakh, securing the winning bid. The prospect of the Taj Mahal being sold and potentially converted into a Hindu temple deeply troubled Fanny Parkes. She stated:

> By what authority does the Governor-general offer the Taj for sale? Has he any right to molest the dead? To sell the tomb raised over an empress, which from its extraordinary beauty is the wonder of the world? It is impossible the Court of Directors can sanction the sale of the tomb for the sake of its marble and gems. They say that a Hindoo wishes to buy the Taj to carry away the marble, and erect a temple to his own idols at Bindrabund![27]

However, widespread outrage erupted among both British and Indians communities, fuelled by fears of communal riots. This mounting pressure compelled the authorities to cancel the tender, ultimately saving the Taj Mahal from being sold.

She also advocated for Indian Muslims when the beautifully inlaid Mughal zenana rooms in the Agra Fort were damaged during their temporary conversion into a kitchen for the reception of British royals. Within the same fort, marble from Turkish baths was sold by the Marquis of Hastings, though the sum obtained was so insignificant that further sales were not considered.

Britishers dining in the Elephanta Caves in 1875, published in *The Graphic*, 1875.[28]

Later, as was the British custom, they organized festivities in front of historical monuments whenever high-ranking official toured India. In the mid-1800s, they even arranged for a dance troupe to perform on the marble platform of the Taj Mahal. Parkes was incensed by the sacrilege, considering it a violation of the sacred nature of the tomb. Her emotions ran high, prompting her to write:

> Can you imagine anything so detestable? European ladies and gentlemen dance quadrilles in front of the tomb! I cannot enter the Taj without feelings of deep devotion: the sacredness of the place, the remembrance of the fallen grandeur of the family of the Emperor, the solemn echoes, the dim light, the beautiful architecture, the exquisite finish and delicacy of the whole... all produce deep and sacred feelings; and I could no more jest or indulge in levity beneath the dome of the Taj, than I could in my prayers.[29]

To be fair, the British inflicted similar damage on all monuments, irrespective of their religious significance. In 1875, they even hosted a dinner in the revered Elephanta Caves in Mumbai in honour of Prince Charles.

Zenana Affairs

Parkes recounted numerous captivating and amusing anecdotes from her experiences within a Muslim zenana:

> Nothing can exceed the quarrels that go on in the zenana, or the complaints the begams make against each other. A common complaint is 'Such a one has been practising witchcraft against me'. If the husband make a present to one wife, if it be only a basket of mangoes, he must make the same exactly to all the other wives to keep the peace. A wife, when in a rage with her husband, if on account of jealousy, often says, I wish I were married to a grasscutter,' i.e. because a grasscutter is so poor that he can only afford to have one wife.[30]

She narrates the observations of one of her close male acquaintances, who found himself the subject of surprise among Muslim women:

> My having been married some thirty or forty years, and never having taken another wife, surprises the Musulmans very much, and the ladies all look upon me as a pattern: they do not admire a system of having three or four rivals, however well pleased the gentlemen may be with the custom.[31]

Painting depicting Charak Pooja.[32]

Charak Pooja and Hook Swinging

She wrote extensively about the Charak Pooja festival, a popular event in Bengal, which she found quite grotesque. Named after the charak tree, it is celebrated in reverence to Shiva and Durga during the Chaitra month as a new year celebration. The festival aims to bring prosperity, eliminate sorrow and, more importantly, aid childless couples in conceiving children. During the festival, a pole made from the charak tree is erected, and devotees, often known as 'charak sannyasis', perform daring acts as part of their devotion. A priest strikes the devotees on their backs until their flesh becomes numb. After that, metal hooks are inserted through their flesh, allowing them to be lifted off the ground with a device. Many partake in ganja (cannabis) to numb the pain. They are then swung in circles for hours while singing traditional Vedic verses and popular folk songs. Overall, it is considered an act of extraordinary merit rather than a penance for sin.

Thousands of people were on the road, dressed in all their gayest attire, to do honour to the festival of the Churuk Pooja, the swinging by hooks. Amongst the crowd, the most remarkable objects were several Voiragee mendicants; their bodies were covered with ashes, their hair clotted with mud and twisted round their heads; they were naked all but a shred of cloth. One man had held up both arms over his head until they had withered and were immoveable, the nails of the clenched fists had penetrated through the back of the hands, and came out on the other side like the claws of a bird.

Hindoos of the lower castes are very fond of this amusement, accidental deaths occasioned by it are reckoned about three percent. Sometimes four men swing together for half an hour; some in penance for their own sins; some for those of others, richer men, who reward their deputies and thus do penance by proxy.[33]

Hook Swinging.[34]

The festival was banned by the British government in 1864 due to its inherent violence. However, even today, it is celebrated with great enthusiasm in many places all over India, as well as in Sri Lanka and Bangladesh.

Cholera Outbreak

In 1833, during an unusually hot year, a cholera outbreak occurred, resulting in hundreds of Hindu deaths each day. Instead of seeking medical attention, many believed it to be a curse from the goddess. Parkes described how, at night, groups of Hindu women would gather in secluded areas with pooja thalis, dancing half-naked in a circle around a nude woman while chanting mantras to appease the goddess. Men avoided venturing into these areas. She noted that such practices were exclusive to Hindus, as Muslims refrained from such superstitions, contending themselves with fervent cries five times a day. The cholera epidemic subsided only after the arrival of the monsoon.[35]

Conclusion

Through their letters, diaries, journals, memoirs, stories, novels, poems, paintings, illustrations and travel writings, female travellers played a huge role in shaping the perceptions of India and its people among the British population back home. These women have greatly contributed to the West's fascination with the mysteries and allure of the East, often providing invaluable information about the empire. Their writings often served as instruments of both propaganda and whitewashing British atrocities.

While some, like Annie Besant, Freda Bedi, Margret Noble and Marjorie Sykes, wrote to admire, empower and inspire people worldwide, sadly, others, such as Fanny Parkes, wrote to undermine, mock and erode Hindu culture. The white women of the British era were indeed products of imperialism, benefitting from substantial race and class privileges. Their roles were crucial in nurturing the Raj during the 'High Noon' of British imperialism. They embodied both femininity through their direct involvement in homemaking and masculinity through their indirect contributions to empire-building. Throughout, these travelling women remained complicit in the unbridled violence of the British era, often justifying it under the pretext of civilizing the natives. In many instances, they were directly involved in perpetrating violence, especially in domestic contexts.

Intent on improving the lives of the 'savages', they flocked to India in thousands, yet ironically, they seemed oblivious to the struggles faced by women back home in Victorian Britain. England remained a land of contradictions, where one woman reigned as monarch and empress, while others of the same gender could be found languishing in prisons due to a lack of legal rights.

There were numerous crippling famines in India from the 1850s until Independence, during which crores of Indians perished. Yet, no British woman raised her voice against such brutal and unnecessary atrocities by the empire. A few, like Maud Diver, even tried to whitewash British crimes and portrayed themselves as victims:

> The real price of empire was not paid by the indigenous people, who suffered the destruction of handicrafts, extraction of impossibly high revenues, blatantly racist judicial and legal systems, as well as incomplete capitalist development, to list a few of the exorbitant costs that India paid.
>
> The real price was being paid by the self-sacrificing men and women of England, so that 'India's gradual movement towards mental and national awakening is the net result of countless seemingly futile, individual struggles, of daily battles, against heat, dust and cholera and that insidious inertia of soul and body that is the moral microbe of the East.[36]

Diver was not the only one to express such sentiments. Many English women deeply entrenched in colonial ideology ended up justifying the Raj. Pamela Hinkson, who visited India in the late 1930s, was another vocal advocate for the empire, believing that the British had made significant sacrifices through colonizing

India. She lamented that 'a failed BA reads newspapers to the illiterates rather than preaching the evils of suttee'.[37]

Norah Hamilton even noted the unintended (and often wasteful) uses of the skills that the British had imparted to the Indians, particularly in nationalist agitations. While imperialism was predominantly driven by men due to its emphasis on conquest and control, women made substantial contributions to the process of building an empire by providing psychological and physical support to their husbands. Some women carved out a niche for themselves by writing memoirs that shed light on contemporary situations. They played a crucial role in upholding the hierarchy of patriarchy, imperialism and capitalism, maintaining the relationships between 'father and children, master and servant, employer and employed'.

The European women were indeed an integral component of the broader imperialist framework, and without their direct and indirect contributions, the empire would not have endured for as long as it did.[38]

Epilogue

All these travellers approached India from diverse perspectives. Moreover, they were separated by centuries, hailed from different regions of Europe and were distant enough, both temporally and geographically, to convey historical significance to their respective observations. Their perceptions were unfiltered, and they arrived as individuals rather than emissaries of their respective rulers, adding further credibility to their accounts. They documented their experiences as they witnessed them.

The travellers' accounts offer valuable insights into India's past eras, serving as important historical documents. Their occasional anti-Hindu sentiments, prevalent throughout their writings, largely stem from their Christian background, as they were unfamiliar with depictions of deities with multiple arms and heads. The Abrahamic religions of Christianity and Islam have historically taught their followers to view others as pagan, heathen or kafir, deserving only of destruction. In this regard, Christians are perceived as slightly more tolerant than Muslims, as they might preserve remnants of pagan cultures in vast museums after eradicating them.

India indeed had extensive trade relations with Southeast Asian countries and even with regions as distant as Rome. The history of communication between Europe and India from ancient times to the medieval era is characterized by intense competition for Indian trade. George Birdwood, in his work, *The Modern Quest and Invention of the Indies*, asserted that 'the history of modern Europe, and emphatically of England, is the history of the quest of the aromatic gum resins and balsams, and condiments and spices, of India, Further India, and the Indian Archipelago'.

In contrast, very few people from India travelled abroad and recorded global events. Bodhidharma, a Buddhist monk credited as the father of Shaolin Kungfu, went to China in the late 5th century but never returned. However, there are hardly any significant travelogues from such journeys, with travellers often focussing solely on their business transactions rather than broader observations. This lack of comprehensive travel accounts contributed to India remaining isolated from global developments, resulting in missed opportunities to benefit from historical knowledge.

During the medieval era, significant military inventions were occurring globally, but Indians remained largely unaware. Developments such as composite bows, horse saddles, chain mail, etc., had the potential to revolutionize warfare. Centuries later, Europeans introduced gunpowder, which the Turks quickly adopted. Babur arrived in India in 1526 with cannons, presenting a formidable challenge to the Delhi sultans, who lacked effective countermeasures.

One of the contributing factors to India's 800-year-old slavery was the absence of Indian travellers and explorers who documented their experiences. This lack of engagement led to a significant oversight during medieval times, leaving India unaware of the dynamic changes occurring in the Islamic world and its military strategies. Perhaps there was an element of overconfidence, believing that nobody could surpass Indian prowess. This oversight is particularly regrettable considering India's historical achievements in establishing Indic empires in Southeast Asia. In contrast, Europe rose to prominence and continues to wield influence globally due to the daring and adventurous explorers of the 15th–17th centuries.

Even today, as the Indian diaspora achieves prominence in political and business circles worldwide, there remains a dearth of discerning travel accounts documenting their experiences.

Notes

Author's Note

1   https://commons.wikimedia.org/wiki/File:Mandeville_cotton.jpg

Chapter 2: Early European Knowledge of India

1   https://en.wikipedia.org/wiki/File:Berenike_Buddha.jpg

2   Yule, H. and A.C. Burnell, 1886, *Hobson-Jobson: The Definitive Glossary of British India*, London: John Murray, p. 331.

3   Oaten, E.F., 1909, *European Travellers in India during the 15th, 16th and 17th Centuries*, New Delhi: Asian Educational Services, pp. 11–12.

4   Ibid.

5   Ibid., p. 12.

6   Agarwal, A., 2020, *Swift Horses Sharp Swords: Medieval Battles Which Shook India*, Delhi: Karmanya Publishers, p. 84.

7   Ball, W., 2016, *Rome in the East: The Transformation of an Empire*, New York: Routledge, p. 141.

8   https://commons.wikimedia.org/wiki/File:Indo-Roman_trade.jpg

9   Guy, J., and V. Tournier, 2023, *Tree and Serpent: Early Buddhist Art in India*, New York: Metropolitan Museum of Art, p. 161.

10 https://en.m.wikipedia.org/wiki/File:Gold_coin_of_Claudius_50_51CE_excavated_in_South_India.jpg

11 https://en.m.wikipedia.org/wiki/File:TrajanCoinAhinposhBuddhist-MonasteryAfghanistan.jpg

12 Oaten, E.F., 1909, *European Travellers in India during the 15th, 16th and 17th Centuries*, New Delhi: Asian Educational Services, p. 11.

13 Casson, L., 1989, *The Periplus Maris Erythraei*, New Jersey: Princeton University Press, p. 14.

14 Bernier, F., 1891, *Travels in the Mogul Empire,* CE *1656–68*, Vol. 1, translated by Irving Brock, Edinburgh: Archibald Constable and Company, p. 263.

15 Ibid., p. 225.

Chapter 3: Prominent Foreign Travellers to India

1   Braudel, F., 1979, *The Wheels of Commerce: Civilisation and Capitalism 15th–18th Century,* p. 169.

Chapter 4: Niccolao Manucci

1   Manucci, N., 1913, *A Pepys of Mogul India,* New York: E.P. Dutton and Company, p. 5.

2   Ibid., p. 31.

3   Manucci, N., 1907, *Storia Do Mogor,* Vol. I, London: John Murray, p. 67.

4   https://en.wikipedia.org/wiki/Niccolao_Manucci#/media/File:Manucci. jpg

5   Eti Agarwal.

6   Manucci, N., 1907, *Storia Do Mogor,* Vol. I, London: John Murray, pp. 68–69.

7   Ibid., p. 96.

8   Ovington, J., 1929, *A Voyage to Surat in the Year 1689,* London: Oxford University Press, p. 147.

9   Eti Agarwal.

10 https://commons.wikimedia.org/wiki/File:The_Battle_of_Samugarh.jpg

11 Sarkar, J., 1912, *History of Aurangzib,* Vols. I and II, Calcutta: Orient Longman Limited, p. 221.

12 https://commons.wikimedia.org/wiki/File:Bolan_Pass_1842.jpg

13 Eraly, A. 2007, *Emperors of the Peacock Throne,* Delhi: Penguin Books, p. 408.

14 Hansen, W., 1986, *The Peacock Throne: The Drama of Mogul India,* New Delhi: Orient Book Distributors, p. 380.

15 Manucci, N., 1989, *Mogul India* or *Storia do Mogor, Vol. 1,* Atlantic Publishers and Distributors, pp. 356–57

16 Manucci, N., 1907, *Storia Do Mogor,* Vol. I, London: John Murray, p. 87.

17 Najmuddin, S.Z., 2005, *Armenia: A Resumé: with Notes on Seth's Armenians in India,* Bloomington: Trafford Publishing, p. 152.

18 https://commons.wikimedia.org/wiki/File:Indian_Single_Leaf_of_Shah_ Sarmad_and_Prince_Dara_Shikoh_-_Walters_W912.jpg

19 Dalrymple, W., 2019, *The Anarchy,* Delhi: Bloomsbury Publishing, p. 79.

20 Manucci, N., 1907, *Storia Do Mogor,* Vol. I, London: John Murray, p. 223.

21 Ibid., p. 221.

22 Ibid., Vol. II, p. 340.

23 Manucci, N., 1913, *A Pepys of Mogul India,* New York: E.P. Dutton and Company, p. 153.

24   Eti Agarwal.

25   Manucci, N., 1907, *Storia Do Mogor*, Vol. II, London: John Murray, p. 212.

26   https://commons.wikimedia.org/wiki/File:Manucci_pulse.jpg

27   Manucci, N., 1913, *A Pepys of Mogul India*, New York: E.P. Dutton and Company, p. 203.

28   Manucci, N., 1907, *Storia Do Mogor*, Vol. II, London: p. 329.

29   Ibid., Vol. III, p. 397.

30   Ibid., Vol. I, p. 188.

31   Ibid., Vol. III, p. 145.

32   Eti Agarwal.

33   Ibid.

34   Manucci, N., 1907, *Storia Do Mogor*, Vol. II, London: John Murray, p. 154.

35   Ibid.

36   Ibid., p. 154.

37   Agarwal, A., 2022, *A Never-Ending Conflict*, Gurgaon: Garuda Prakashan, pp. 212–13.

38   Eti Agarwal.

39   Subrahmanyam, S., 2011, *Three Ways to Be Alien: Travails and Encounters in the Early Modern World*, Massachusetts: Brandeis University Press, p. 154.

40   Manucci, N., 1705, *Libro Nero*, Venice: Biblioteca Marciana, p. 86.

41   Manucci, N., 1907, *Storia Do Mogor*, Vol. II, London: John Murray, p. 329.

Chapter 5: William Hawkins

1   https://en.m.wikipedia.org/wiki/File:William_Hawkins.jpg

2   Keay, J., 1993, *The Honourable Company: A History of the English East India Company*, London: HarperCollins Publishers, p. 77.

3   Lane-Poole, S., 1906, *History of India*, Vol. IV, London: The Grolier Society, p. 58.

4   Habib, I., 1963, *The Agrarian System of Mughal India, 1556–1707*, London: Asia Publishing House, pp. 75–76.

5   Dalrymple, W., 2019, *The Anarchy*, Delhi: Bloomsbury Publishing, p. 55.

6   Melo, J.V., 2023, *The Writings of Antoni de Montserrat at the Mughal Court*, Leiden: Brill, p. 58.

7   Dalrymple, W., 2019, *The Anarchy*, Delhi: Bloomsbury Publishing, p. 55.

8   Lane-Poole, S., 1906, *History of India: Mediaeval India from the Mohammedan Conquest to the Reign of Akbar the Great*, London: The Grolier Society, p. 62.

9   Bailey, G.A., 1998, 'The Indian Conquest of Catholic Art', *Art Journal*, 57:1, pp. 24–30, accessed 28 February 2024.

10 https://en.wikipedia.org/wiki/File:Jahangir_holding_the_picture_of_Madonna_-_Google_Art_Project.jpg

11 Manucci, N., 1907, *Storia Do Mogor, Vol. 1*, London: John Murray, pp. 158–161.

12 Foster, W. (ed.), 1921, *Early Travels in India*, London: Oxford University Press, p. 70.

13 Ibid., p. 116.

14 Ibid., p. 85.

15 Markham, C.R., 1878, *The Hawkins Voyages*, London: Hakluyt Society, p. 15.

16 Foster, W. (ed.), 1921, *Early Travels in India*, London: Oxford University Press, p. 104.

17 Mitra, S., 2005, *Gir Forest and the Saga of the Asiatic Lion*, Delhi: Indus Publishing, p. 37.

18 Lane-Poole, S., 1906, *History of India*, Vol. IV, London: The Grolier Society, p. 66.

19 Mukhoty, I., 2018, *Daughters of the Sun: Empresses, Queens and Begums of the Mughal Empire*, Delhi: Aleph Book Company, p. 147.

20 Lane-Poole, S., 1906, *History of India*, Vol. IV, London: The Grolier Society, p. 67.

21 https://commons.wikimedia.org/wiki/File:The_East_offering_its_riches_to_Britannia_-_Roma_Spiridone,_1778_-_BL_Foster_245.jpg

22 https://commons.wikimedia.org/wiki/File:SIR_THOMAS_STOOD_BEFORE_THE_MOGUL.gif

23 https://en.m.wikipedia.org/wiki/File:Shah_%27Alam_conveying_the_grant_of_the_Diwani_to_Lord_Clive.jpg

24 Sarkar, J. (trans.), 1952, 'The Muzaffarnama of Karam Ali', in *Bengal Nawabs*, Calcutta, p. 63.

25 Khan, G.H., 1902, *Seir Mutaqherin, 1790-94*, Vol. 3, Calcutta: T.D. Chatterjee, pp. 9–10.

26 Carson, P., 2012, *The East India Company and Religion, 1698-1858*, Woodbridge: The Boydell Press, p. 19.

27 Poynder, J., 1844, *Literary Extracts*, Vol. 1, London: John Hatchard and Son, p. 268.

28 Sramek, J., 2011, *Gender, Morality, and Race in Company India, 1765-1858*, New York: Palgrave Macmillan, p. 17.

29 Davis, M., 2002, *Late Victorian Holocausts: El Niño Famines and the Making of the Third World*, London: Verso, p. 22.

Chapter 6: Jean-Baptiste Tavernier

1   Ibid.

2   https://commons.wikimedia.org/wiki/File:Jean-Baptist_Tavernier,_by_
    Nicolas_de_Largilli%C3%A8re.jpg

3   https://commons.wikimedia.org/wiki/File:Frans_Hogenberg,_The_St._
    Bartholomew%27s_Day_massacre,_circa_1572.jpg

4   Tavernier, J.B., 1889, *Travels in India*, translated by V. Ball, London:
    Macmillan and Co., p. ii.

5   Yule, H., 2003, *The Travels of Marco Polo*, Vol. II, New York: Dover
    Publications, p. 361.

6   Eti Agarwal.

7   https://commons.wikimedia.org/wiki/File:Plan_exact_de_Gomron_
    ou_du_Bandar_Abassi,_de_l'Isle_d'Ormus_et_des_Isles_voisines_-_
    Tavernier_Jean_Baptiste_-_1677.jpg

8   Wise, R., 2009, *The French Blue*, Massachusetts: Brunswick House Press,
    p. 209.

9   Agarwal, A., 2022, *A Never-ending Conflict*, Gurgaon: Garuda Prakashan,
    pp. 167–68.

10 Sharan, I., 1991, *The Myth of Saint Thomas and the Mylapore Shiva Temple*,
    New Delhi: Voice of India, p. 80.

11 Tavernier, J.B., 1889, *Travels in India*, translated by V. Ball, London:
    Macmillan and Co., p. 184.

12 Eti Agarwal.

13 Tavernier, J.B., 1889, *Travels in India*, translated by V. Ball, London:
    Macmillan and Co., p. 184.

14 https://en.m.wikipedia.org/wiki/File:Mirjumla.jpg

15 Sarkar, J., 1951, *The Life of Mir Jumla*, Calcutta: Thacker, Spink & Co.,
    p. 77.

16 https://commons.wikimedia.org/wiki/File:Fabled_diamond_mines.jpg

17 Sarkar, J., 1951, *The Life of Mir Jumla*, Calcutta: Thacker, Spink & Co.,
    p. 18.

18 Ibid., p. 80.

19 https://commons.wikimedia.org/wiki/File:Masulipatam_mg_8557.jpg

20 Tavernier, J.B., 1678, *The Six Voyages of John Baptista Tavernier, Baron of
    Aubonne through Turky, into Persia and the East-Indies, for the Space of Forty
    Years*, London: Robert Littlebury, p. 46.

21 Fanthorpe, P., 2002, *The World's Most Mysterious Objects*, Toronto:
    Hounslow Book.

22 Eti Agarwal.

23 https://commons.wikimedia.org/wiki/File:Schets_van_de_ruwe_Hope_diamant_door_Tavernier.jpg

24 Eti Agarwal.

25 Kurin, R., 2007, *Hope Diamond: The Legendary History of a Cursed Gem*, New York: HarperCollins, p. 22.

26 Boissoneault, L., 30 August 2017, 'The True Story of the Koh-i-Noor Diamond—and Why the British Won't Give it Back', *Smithsonian Magazine*, last accessed on 28 February 2024.

27 Kurin, R., 2007, Hope Diamond: The Legendary *History of a Cursed Gem*, New York: HarperCollins.

28 https://naturalhistory.si.edu/explore/collections/hope-diamond-history

29 Lane-Poole, S., 1908, *Aurangzib and the Decay of the Mughal Empire*, Oxford: Clarendon Press, p. 65.

30 Lane-Poole, S., 1903, *Mediaeval India from the Mohammedan Conquest to the Reign of Akbar the Great*, London: The Grolier Society, p. 102.

31 Ibid., p. 96.

32 Ibid.

33 Tavernier, J.B., 1678, *The Six Voyages of John Baptista Tavernier, Baron of Aubonne through Turky, into Persia and the East-Indies, for the Space of Forty Years*, London: Robert Littlebury, p. 161.

34 Sarkar, J., 1951, *The Life of Mir Jumla*, Calcutta: Thacker, Spink & Co., p. 50.

35 Tavernier, J.B., 1889, *Travels in India*, translated by V. Ball, London: Macmillan and Co., p. 290.

36 Goel, S., 1991, *Hindu Temples: What Happened to Them?*, New Delhi: Voice of India, p. 187.

37 Tavernier, J.B., 2000, *Travels in India*, Vol. III, edited by W. Crooke, Low Price Publications, p. 137; quoted from Jain, M. (ed.), 2011, *The India They Saw: Foreign Accounts*, Vol. III, New Delhi: Ocean Books, Chapter 15.

38 https://commons.wikimedia.org/wiki/File:Banyans_Yogis.jpeg

39 Tavernier, J.B., 1889, *Travels in India*, translated by V. Ball, London: Macmillan and Co., p. 265.

40 Twain, M., 1897, *Following the Equator*, New York: Harper & Brothers Publishers, p. 165.

41 Jean-Baptiste Tavernier, J.B., 1678, *The Six Voyages of John Baptista Tavernier, Baron of Aubonne through Turky, into Persia and the East-Indies, for the Space of Forty Years*, (London: Robert Littlebury, 1678), p. 161.

42 Sadasivan, B., 2011, *The Dancing Girl: A History of Early India*, Singapore: Institute of Southeast Asian Studies, p. 293.

Chapter 7: Mark Twain

1 commons.wikimedia.org/wiki/File:Mark_Twain_by_AF_Bradley.jpg
2 Twain, M., 1897, *Following the Equator*, New York: Harper & Brothers Publishers, p. 355.
3 commons.wikimedia.org/wiki/File:Parsee_Tower_of_Silence,_Bombay.jpg
4 Twain, M., 1897, *Following the Equator*, New York: Harper & Brothers Publishers, p. 58.
5 Ibid., p. 26.
6 Ibid., p. 248.
7 Ibid., p. 232.
8 Eti Agarwal.
9 Twain, M., 1897, *Following the Equator*, New York: Harper & Brothers Publishers, p. 174.
10 Ibid., p. 175.
11 Ibid., p. 177.
12 Ibid., p. 178.
13 Ibid., p. 194.
14 Ibid., p. 198.
15 Ibid., p. 200.
16 Ibid., p. 202.
17 Ibid., p. 201.
18 commons.wikimedia.org/wiki/File:The_Black_hole%27_june_20_1756.jpg
19 Twain, M., 1897, *Following the Equator*, New York: Harper & Brothers Publishers, p. 219.
20 Ibid., pp. 245–47.
21 Ibid., p. 250.
22 Ibid., p. 261.
23 https://en.m.wikipedia.org/wiki/File:The_Relief_of_Lucknow,_1857_by_Thomas_Jones_Barker.jpg
24 Malleson, G.B., 1858, *The History of the Indian Mutiny*, London: William H. Allen and Co., p. 245.
25 Nath, I., 2022, *Memsahibs: British Women in Colonial India*, London: Hurst & Company, p. 238.
26 Twain, M., 1897, *Following the Equator*, New York: Harper & Brothers Publishers, p. 261.
27 Twain, M., 1897, *Following the Equator*, New York: Harper & Brothers Publishers, p. 269.

28   Ibid., p. 145.

29   Sleeman, W.H., 1858, *A Journey Through the Kingdom of Oude in 1849–50*, Vol. 1, London: Richard Bentley, pp. 206–22.

30   https://commons.wikimedia.org/wiki/File:Sanichar-cropped.png

31   Twain, M., 1897, *Following the Equator*, New York: Harper & Brothers Publishers, p. 136.

32   Ibid., pp. 113–20.

33   https://en.wikipedia.org/wiki/File:The_Thugs_Worshipping_Kalee_(1850,_p._98)_-_Copy.jpg

34   Wagner, K., 2007, *Thuggee: Banditry and the British in Early Nineteenth-Century India*, London: Palgrave, p. 141.

35   Twain, M., 1897, *Following the Equator*, New York: Harper & Brothers Publishers, p. 125.

36   Wagner, K., 2007, *Thuggee: Banditry and the British in Early Nineteenth-Century India*, London: Palgrave, p. 92.

37   https://en.m.wikipedia.org/wiki/File:Thugs_Strangling_Traveller.jpg

38   Rid, S., 1930, 'Martin Markall, Beadle of Bridewell', in *The Elizabethan Underworld*, A.V. Judges (ed.), London: George Routledge, pp. 415–16.

39   Twain, M., 1897, *Following the Equator*, New York: Harper & Brothers Publishers, p. 197.

40   Ibid., p. 85.

41   Ibid., p. 160.

Chapter 8: Afanasy Nikitin

1   Eti Agarwal.

2   Nikitin, A., 2000, *Voyage to India*, translated by Count Wielhorski, Ontario: In Parentheses publications, p. 3.

3   Polo, M., 1958, *The Travels of Marco Polo*, translated by Robert Latham, London, Penguin Books, p. 264.

4   Agarwal, A., 2020, *Swift Horses Sharp Swords: Medieval Battles Which Shook India*, Delhi: Karmanya Publishers, p. 134.

5   Nikitin, A., 1960, *Journey beyond Three Seas*, Moscow: Raduga Publishers, p. 109.

6   Richard, Maj. H. (ed.), 1857, *India in the Fifteenth Century*, London: Hakluyt Society, pp. 198–230.

7   Maxwell, M.J., September 2006, 'Afanasii Nikitin: An Orthodox Russian's Spiritual Voyage in the Dar al-Islam, 1468–75', *Journal of World History*, Vol. 17, No. 3, p. 252.

8   Nikitin, A., 1960, *Journey beyond Three Seas*, Moscow: Raduga Publishers, p. 111.

9   Lenhoff, G. and J. Martin, 1989, 'The Commercial and Cultural Context of Afanasij Nikitin's Journey beyond Three Seas', *Jahrbücher für Geschichte Osteuropas*, p. 330.

10   Chaudhuri, K.N., 1985, *Trade and Civilization in the Indian Ocean*, Cambridge: Cambridge University Press, pp. 100–01.

11   Eti Agarwal.

12   Nikitin, A., 2000, *Voyage to India*, translated by Count Wielhorski, Ontario: In Parentheses publications, p. 111.

13   Ibid., p. 9.

14   Ibid., p. 61.

15   Ibid., p. 114.

16   Ibid., p. 116.

17   Maxwell, M.J., 2006, *Afanasii Nikitin: An Orthodox Russian's Spiritual Voyage in the Dar al-Islam, 1468-1475*, The Pennsylvania State University, p. 1.

18   Nikitin, A., 2000, *Voyage to India*, translated by Count Wielhorski, Ontario: In Parentheses publications, p. 6.

19   en.wikipedia.org/wiki/File:Journey_Beyond_Three_Seas_Indian_poster.jpg

20   commons.wikimedia.org/wiki/File:Afansiy_Nikitin_memorial_theodosia.jpg

21   India Post.

Chapter 9: Fanny Parkes and Other British Women Explorers

1   Tacitus, C., 'Speech by Caecina Severus', *Annals III*, 33.

2   Hyam, R., 1991, *Empire and Sexuality: The British Experience*, Manchester: Manchester University Press, p. 115.

3   Brown, S.S., 1878, *Home Letters Written from India 1828–41*, London: C.F. Roworth, p. 17.

4   Hyam, R., 1991, *Empire and Sexuality: The British Experience*, Manchester: Manchester University Press, p. 125.

5   Ghose, I., 2007, *The Memsahib Myth: Englishwomen in Colonial India*, New York: Palgrave Macmillan, p. 107.

6   Ballhatchet, K., 1980, *Race, Sex and Class*, New York: St Martin's Press, p. 5.

7   Noble, M., 1904, *The Web of Indian Life*, London: William Heinemann, p. 68.

8   commons.wikimedia.org/wiki/File:Joshua_Reynolds__Tysoe_Hancock_
      and_his_Family_with_an_Indian_Maid_-_WGA19338.jpg

9   Blunt, W.S., 1885, *Ideas about India,* London: Kegan Paul, Trench & Co.
      p. 47.

10   Hyam, R., 1991, *Empire and Sexuality: The British Experience*, Manchester:
      Manchester University Press, p. 119.

11   Ibid., p. 118.

12   Gaughan, J.M., 2013, *The Incumberances: British Women in India 1615–
      1856,* New York: Oxford University Press, p. 45.

13   Ghose, I., 1998, *Women Travellers in Colonial India: The Power of Female
      Gaze*, Delhi: Oxford University Press, p. 66.

14   Diver, M., 1909, *The Englishwoman in India*, London: William Blackwood
      and Sons, p. 120.

15   Wingfield-Stratford, B., 1922, *India and the English*, London: Jonathan
      Cape, p. 122.

16   Hamilton, N.R., 1915, *Through Wonderful India and beyond*, London:
      Holden & Hardingham Adelphi, p. 259.

17   Hinkson, P., 1941, *Indian Harvest*, London: Collins, p. 256.

18   Besant, A., 1940, 'Women in India' (1917), in *The India That Shall Be*,
      Madras: Theosophical Publishing House, p. 254.

19   commons.wikimedia.org/wiki/File:Bharat_Mata_by_Abanindranath_
      Tagore.jpg

20   theguardian.com/books/2019/may/17/she-merchants-buccaneers-
      gentlewomen-british-women-india-katie-hickman-review

21   Butler, A., 1954, *Portrait of Josephine Butler*, London: Faber & Faber, p. 196.

22   https://commons.wikimedia.org/wiki/File:Sister_Nivedita_1968_stamp_
      of_India.jpg

23   Sister Nivedita, 1947, *The Complete Works of Sister Nivedita*, Vol. II, Kolkata:
      Advaita Ashrama, p. 470.

24   Unknown photographer, Mussories, 1875.

25   https://commons.wikimedia.org/wiki/File:Freda_Bedi_and_Baba_Pyare_
      Lal_Bedi,_at_Nishat_Bagh,_Srinagar,_1948.jpg

26   Parkes, F., 1850, *Wanderings of a Pilgrim in Search of the Picturesque during
      Four and Twenty Years in the East with Revelations of Life in the Zenana*, Vol.
      I, London: Pelham Richardson.

27   Parkes, F., 2003, *Begums, Thugs and Englishmen*, Delhi: Penguin, p. 121.

28   https://commons.wikimedia.org/wiki/File:%22The_Prince_of_Wales_
      Dining_in_the_Caves_of_Elephanta,_Bombay,_from_a_sketch_by_
      one_of_our_special_artists,%22_from_The_Graphic,_1875.jpg

29   Parkes, F., 1850, *Wanderings of a Pilgrim in Search of the Picturesque during Four and Twenty Years in the East with Revelations of Life in the Zenana*, Vol. I, London: Pelham Richardson, p. 355.

30   Ibid., pp. 230–31.

31   Ibid., p. 231.

32   commons.wikimedia.org/wiki/File:Charak-Indian_Museum,_Kolkata_ R.13413.jpg

33   Parkes, F., 1850, *Wanderings of a Pilgrim in Search of the Picturesque during Four and Twenty Years in the East with Revelations of Life in the Zenana*, Vol. I, London: Pelham Richardson, p. 27.

34   commons.wikimedia.org/wiki/File:Fishing_Hook_Monk_at_Gajan.jpg

35   Parkes, F., 1850, *Wanderings of a Pilgrim in Search of the Picturesque during Four and Twenty Years in the East with Revelations of Life in the Zenana*, Vol. I, London: Pelham Richardson, pp. 281–82.

36   Diver, M., 1909, *The Englishwoman in India*, London: William Blackwood and Sons, pp. 128–29.

37   Hinkson, P., 1941, *Indian Harvest*, London: Collins, p. 258.

38   Hall, C., 2000, *Cultures of Empire: Colonizers in Britain and the Empire in the Nineteenth and Twentieth Centuries*, New York: Routledge, p. 239.

References

Agarwal, A., 2020, *Swift Horses Sharp Swords: Medieval Battles Which Shook India*, New Delhi: Karmanya Publishers

——, 2022, *A Never-ending Conflict: Episodes from Indic Resistance*, New Delhi: Garuda Prakashan.

——, 2024, *Temple Treasures*, Hubli: Subbu.

Al-Biruni, A.R., 1941, *Kitāb al-Hind*, Delhi: Anjuman Taraqqi Urdu (Hind).

Banerjee, R., 2024, *India in Early Modern English Travel Writings: Protestantism, Enlightenment, and Toleration*, New Delhi: Manohar Publishers & Distributors.

Bernier, F., 2023, *Travels in the Mogul Empire*, New Delhi: Atlantic Publishers and Distributors Pvt. Ltd.

Bracciolini, P., 1857, *India in the Fifteenth Century (Travels of Nicolo Conti)*, London: Hakluyt Society.

Bredsdorff, A., 2009, *Trials and Travels of Willem Leyel: An Account of the Danish East India Company in Tranquebar*, Denmark: Museum Tusculanum Press.

Das Gupta, J.N., 2018, *India in the Seventeenth Century as Depicted by European Travellers*, London: Forgotten Books.

Della Valle, E.G.P., 2020, *The Travels of Pietro Della Valle in India*, New Delhi: Gyan Publishing House.

Faxian, 1886, *A Record of Buddhistic Kingdoms*, England: Oxford Clarendon Press.

Fisher, M.H, 2007, *Visions of Mughal India: An Anthology of European Travel Writing*, London: I.B. Tauris.

——, 2005, *Counterflows to Colonialism Indian Travellers and Settlers in Britain*, Ranikhet: Permanent Black.

Foster, W., 2017, *Early Travels in India*, New Delhi: Munshiram Manoharlal Publishers Pvt. Ltd.

Ghose, I., 1998, *Women Travellers in Colonial India: The Power of the Female Gaze*, New Delhi: OUP India.

Ghosh, B., 2017, *Gazing at Neighbours: Travels Along the Line That Partitioned India*, Kolkata: Tranquebar.

Goodwin, J., 2013, *The Gunpowder Gardens* or *A Time for Tea: Travels through China and India in Search of Tea*, UK: Argonaut Books.

Hagglund, B. (ed.), 2020, 'The Life of Mrs Sherwood (1854)', in *Women's Travel Writings in India 1777–1854, Vol. IV*, USA: Routledge.

Haksar, N., 2013, *Across the Chicken Neck: Travels in Northeast India*, New Delhi: Rupa Publications.

Hodges, W., 2010, *Travels in India in Years 1780, 1781, 1782 & 1783*, Michigan: Gale Ecco.

Huntingford, G.W.B. (ed.), 2010, *Periplus of the Erythraean Sea*, London: Hakluyt Society.

Jain, M., 2011, *The India They Saw (Vol 1-4): Continuing the Exploration of India*, New Delhi: Prabhat Prakashan.

Lewis, N., 1993, *A Goddess in the Stones: Travels in India*, New York: Henry Holt & Co.

Mackintosh-Smith, T., 2012, *Travels with a Tangerine: A Journey in the Footnotes of Ibn Battutah*, UK: John Murray.

——, (trans.), 2016, *The Travels of Ibn Battuta*, London: Macmillan Collector's Library.

Major, R.H. (ed.), 2010, *India in the Fifteenth Century*, London: Cambridge University Press.

Manucci, N., 2022, *Mogul India* or *Storia Do Mogor*, New Delhi: Atlantic Publishers and Distributors.

Nath, R., 2020, *India as Seen by William Finch (1608-11 A.D)*, USA: Independently Published.

Nayar, P.K., 2020, *Indian Travel Writing in the Age of Empire: 1830–1940*, New Delhi: Bloomsbury India.

Newby, E., 2010, *A Short Walk in the Hindu Kush*, London: Harper Press.

Nichols, A., 2013, *Ctesias: On India*, India: Bloomsbury Academic.

Oaten, E.F., 2020, *European Travellers in India during the Fifteenth, Sixteenth, and Seventeenth Centuries*, New Delhi: Gyan Publishing House.

Oberoi, R., 2023, *Kanchenjunga Whispers: Legends and Tales from the Elgin*, New Delhi: Rupa Publications.

Paes, D. and F. Nunes, 1897, *Chronica dos reis de Bisnaga (Chronicle of the Kings of Bisnaga [Vijayanagara])*, Lisboa: Imprensa Nacional.

Phillpotts, B.S. (ed.), 2010, *The Life of the Icelander Jón Ólafsson, Traveller to India*, London: Hakluyt Society.

Polo, M., 2004, *Travels of Marco Polo*, New York: Penguin.

Prasad, R.C., 1980, *Early English Travellers in India*, New Delhi: Motilal Banarsidas.

Roberts, J., 2015, *Three-Quarters of a Footprint: Travels in South India*, New Delhi: Aleph Book Company.

Rousselet, L., 2012, *India and Its Native Princes: Travels in Central India and in the Presidencies of Bombay and Bengal*, Delhi: Asian Educational Services.

Samanth, S., 2009, *Following Fish: Travels around the Indian Coast*, New Delhi: Penguin India.

Schnepel, B. and T. Sen (eds), 2019, *Travelling Pasts: The Politics of Cultural Heritage in the Indian Ocean World*, Leiden: Brill Academic Pub.

Schonberg, Baron E.V., 2012, *Travels in India and Kashmir*, Srinagar: Gulshan Books.

Schwanbeck, E.A., 2012, *Megasthenes Indica*, New York: Nabu Press

Seely, J.B., 2014, *The Road Book of India or East Indian Travellers Guide through the Presidencies of Bengal, Madras, and Bombay*, New York: Nabu Press.

Theroux, P., 2008, *Great Railway Bazaar*, London: Penguin.

Tsang, H., *Si-yu-ki: Buddhist Records of the Western World*, London: Trubner & Co.

Urson, M., 2015, *Way out in India: Travels in a Curious Land*, California: Createspace Independent Pub.

Vincent, W., 2010, *Voyage of Nearchus, and the Periplus of the Erythrean Sea*, England: Read Books.

Watters, T., 2018, *On Yuan Chwang's Travels in India, 629-645 A.D.*, London: Forgotten Books.

Whitman, B., 2008, *Wanderlust and Lipstick: For Women Traveling to India*, Dispatch Travels.

About the Author

Amit Agarwal has an engineering degree from the University of Roorkee (now IIT Roorkee). Currently, he is on a sabbatical, taking out time for a subject he is passionate about—history.

His first book, *Swift Horses, Sharp Swords*, deals with medieval Islamic invasions. It's been translated into Hindi. In 2022, he published his second book, *A Never-ending Conflict*, focussing on Indian history again. His next, *Temple Treasure: A Journey through Time*, which explores the history of temples, is set to be published soon.

He is an avid marathoner and mountaineer. He is also passionate about teaching and once taught history at Amrita Vishwa Vidyapeetham. In his spare time, he teaches maths to underprivileged children.